Lawrence Lewis

A History of the Bank of North America

Prepared at theRrequest of the President and Directors

Lawrence Lewis

A History of the Bank of North America
Prepared at theRrequest of the President and Directors

ISBN/EAN: 9783743325128

Manufactured in Europe, USA, Canada, Australia, Japa

Cover: Foto ©ninafisch / pixelio.de

Manufactured and distributed by brebook publishing software (www.brebook.com)

Lawrence Lewis

A History of the Bank of North America

A HISTORY

OF THE

BANK OF NORTH AMERICA,

THE FIRST BANK CHARTERED IN THE
UNITED STATES.

PREPARED AT THE REQUEST OF THE PRESIDENT AND DIRECTORS, BY
LAWRENCE LEWIS, Jr.

PHILADELPHIA:
J. B. LIPPINCOTT & CO.
1882.

PREFACE.

THE occurrence of the centennial anniversary of the incorporation of the Bank of North America affords a fitting opportunity to present to the public an historical sketch of the origin and career of that venerable institution.

Unlike most of the banks in this country, its early annals abound in interesting features. It was the first bank chartered in the United States. Organized at a very critical period of the Revolution, almost wholly from a patriotic desire to sustain the feeble credit of Congress, its first transactions are most intimately connected with the financial operations of the National Government. By its aid troops were levied, arms and ammunition obtained, supplies furnished to the patriot army, and the expenses of the various departments of Government defrayed. Some of the most prominent financiers of Revolutionary times were numbered among its directors or supporters. Nor were these the only distinguishing features which marked its early career. The granting of its charter by Congress first raised the question as to the existence of implied powers in that body. The annulling of its State franchises by the vote of the Assembly induced the first discussion as to the capacity of a legislative body to take such action. While the propriety of encouraging or prohibiting the system of banking in this country was first mooted in connection with its operations. All these subjects will be found treated of at some length in the following pages. The later history of the bank presents fewer points of interest to the general reader. To give an adequate idea of the scope and character of its operations the financial history of the nation would have to be passed in review, a gigantic task which yet remains to be performed, and which is, of course, quite beyond the limits of the present undertaking. No more has, therefore, been attempted than to sketch in rough outline those events in the history of the institution which seem best calculated to illustrate the principles and policy by which it has been constantly guided.

In some of the important financial crises through which this nation has passed, the Bank of North America has adopted a course diametrically opposed to that pursued by most of the banking institutions of the country. As a rule, the wisdom of the counsels by which it was guided has been fully justified by the event. Of this no better proof can be required than its great and constant prosperity. During the century of its existence it has never passed its semi-annual dividend, except upon five occasions, and then only during a panic unexampled in its magnitude and in the disastrous effects it produced upon the community.

Other features in the later history of the bank have seemed worthy of note. The terms of its various charters, the election and resignation of its presidents, the mode and extent of the assistance afforded by it to the United States Government during the Rebellion, such are some of the topics which, though they may prove dull to the general reader, will be, it is hoped, of some interest to those concerned in the institution.

In the Appendix will be found an accurate list of the officers of the bank, chronologically arranged. This has been carefully compiled from the original archives in the bank's possession. To this have been added such documents connected with the history of the institution as it is believed will best illustrate the text of the narrative.

L. L., Jr.

December, 1881.

CONTENTS.

Preface 3

CHAPTER I.
1763–1780.

Early Views as to Banking in the United States—Review of the Financial Policy of the American Revolution—Hamilton's Scheme for a National Bank—Financial Condition of the Country in 1780—Organization of the Pennsylvania Bank in June, 1780—Character and Extent of its Operations—Its Dissolution 13

CHAPTER II.
1781.

Financial Condition of the Country in 1781—Ratification of the Articles of Confederation in March, 1781—Appointment of Robert Morris as Superintendent of Finance in February, 1781—Morris's Plan for a National Bank—Action of Congress in Reference thereto—Reasons for establishing a National Bank—The Subscriptions to the Undertaking—The Organization of the Bank of North America in November, 1781—Thomas Willing elected President—The Ordinance of Incorporation passed by Congress December 31, 1781 . . . 24

CHAPTER III.

1782-1784.

The Bank of North America begins its Operations on January 7, 1782—Circular Letter of the Superintendent of Finance announcing this Fact to the Governors of the various States—Early Difficulties experienced by the Bank—Stories relating to it circulated by its Enemies—Rapid Success of the Institution—Recognition of its Existence by Connecticut, Rhode Island, and Massachusetts in January and March, 1782—A Charter granted to it by the Assembly of Pennsylvania on March 26, 1782—Opposition to Mr. Willing on Account of alleged Disloyalty—Assistance afforded by the Bank to the National Government—Assistance afforded by it to the State of Pennsylvania—Assistance afforded by it to the City of Philadelphia—Proposed Establishment of the Bank of Pennsylvania in 1784—Abandonment of the Scheme in Consequence of the Increase in the Capital Stock of the Bank of North America—Subscriptions to the New Stock . . 37

CHAPTER IV.

1785-1788.

Pennsylvania Paper Currency—Popular Demand for the issuing thereof in 1785—Attitude of the Bank of North America adverse to the Scheme—Growing Unpopularity of the Bank —Petitions presented to the Assembly praying for a Repeal of its Charter—Arguments for and against the Bank—The State Charter annulled on September 13, 1785—Views of the Directors as to this Action—Continuance of the Bank's Operations—A Charter granted to the Bank by the State of Delaware on February 2, 1786—Attempts to obtain a Repeal of the Annulling Act—A New Charter granted by the State of Pennsylvania on March 17, 1787— Provisions of the Charter—Prosperity of the Institution—Establishment of other Banks 54

CHAPTER V.

1789-1809.

The Constitution of the United States goes into effect in March, 1789—Hamilton's Treasury Report of 1790—Reasons for the Establishment of the Bank of the United States—The Bank of North America unable and unwilling to discharge the Functions of such an Institution—Resignation of Thomas Willing as President in 1792—Election of John Nixon as President—Business of the Bank in 1792—Establishment of the Bank of Pennsylvania in 1793—The Whiskey Insurrection of 1794—Business of the Bank in 1794 and 1795—The Yellow Fever of 1798—Temporary Removal of the Bank to Germantown—Renewal of the Charter in 1799—Increase in the Number of Banking Institutions—Reform in the Bank's Method of transacting Business effected in 1806—Establishment of the Surplus Fund in 1809—Death of John Nixon and Election of John Morton as President in 1809   75

CHAPTER VI.

1810-1846.

Expiration of the Charter of the First Bank of the United States—The Bank of North America Petitions Congress for the Renewal in 1810—Failure to obtain a Renewal from Congress—The War of 1812—Assistance afforded by the Bank to the Government during the War—The Panic of 1814—Policy of the Bank during the Panic—Renewal of the Bank's Charter in 1814—Establishment of the Second Bank of the United States—End of the Panic in 1817—Resignation of John Morton from the Presidency in 1822 and Election of Henry Nixon in his place—Renewal of the Charter in 1825—Terms of the New Charter—Sale of the Bank Shares in 1825—Efforts to obtain a Renewal of the Charter of the Second Bank of the United States in 1832—Attitude of the Bank of North America—Failure of the Efforts—Change in the Method of Transacting the Bank's Business between

CONTENTS.

1830 and 1835—The Congressional Charter Null and Void—Failure of Efforts to obtain an Increase of the Capital Stock in 1835—The Panic of 1837—Suspension of Specie Payments—Policy of the Bank of North America—Death of Henry Nixon in 1840, and Election of John Richardson as President—Resumption of Specie Payments in January, 1841—Failure of the Bank of the United States in February, 1841—Renewed Suspension of Specie Payments—The "Relief Act" of May 4, 1841—Refusal of the Bank of North America to accept its Terms—Views of the Bank as to Resumption—Resumption effected in March, 1842—Dangerous Position of the Bank in 1842—Reduction of its Capital in 1843—Restoration of the Capital to its old Volume in 1845—Renewal of the Charter in 1846—Provisions of the New Charter 86

CHAPTER VII.

1847–1882.

Erection of the present Banking-House in 1847—Renewal of the Charter in 1855—The Panic of 1857—Resignation of John Richardson from the Presidency in 1857—Election of James N. Dickson, and his Resignation in 1860—Election of Thomas Smith as President—The War of the Rebellion—Assistance afforded to the Government by the Bank from 1861 to 1864—Loyalty of the Bank—Its Reorganization as a National Bank in 1864—Retention of its Old Title without the usual Prefix "National"—Conclusion . . . 110

APPENDIX.

List of the Presidents, Cashiers, and Directors of the Bank of North America 119
Plan of the Bank of North America submitted to Congress May 17, 1781 . 127
An Ordinance to Incorporate the Subscribers to the Bank of North America, passed by Congress December 31, 1781 130

CONTENTS.

	PAGE
Alphabetical List of the First Subscribers to the Bank of North America	133
Second Subscription to the Bank of North America authorized January 12, 1784	136
Second Subscription to the Bank of North America continued and extended on March 1, 1784	140
Correspondence between the Comptroller of the Currency and the President of the Bank in 1864, relative to the Retention by the Bank of its Old Title on becoming a National Bank	148
Dividends paid by the Bank of North America from 1782 to the Present Time	152

LIST OF ILLUSTRATIONS.

	PAGE
PORTRAIT OF ROBERT MORRIS . . . . *Frontispiece.*	
PORTRAIT OF THOMAS WILLING	34
FAC-SIMILES OF BANK NOTES 1789 AND 1815	75
PORTRAIT OF JOHN NIXON	80
FAC-SIMILES OF BANK NOTES 179 AND 1826	82
PORTRAIT OF JOHN MORTON . . .	85
PORTRAIT OF HENRY NIXON	90
PORTRAIT OF JOHN RICHARDSON	97
PORTRAIT OF JAMES N. DICKSON	113
FAC-SIMILES OF BANK NOTES 1862 AND 1864	115
PORTRAIT OF THOMAS SMITH	118

A HISTORY

OF

THE BANK OF NORTH AMERICA.

CHAPTER I.

1763-1780.

Early Views as to Banking in the United States—Review of the Financial Policy of the American Revolution—Hamilton's Scheme for a National Bank—Financial Condition of the Country in 1780—Organization of the Pennsylvania Bank in June, 1780—Character and Extent of its Operations—Its Dissolution.

THE system of banking has taken its rise in this country within comparatively recent times. In early colonial days the Provincial Governments were carried on with too much economy and simplicity to require the aid of banking capital. Nor were the demands of the business world more pressing. Merchants could generally furnish each other with the loans and discounts necessary to carry on their affairs. A convenient circulating

1763 medium was afforded by bills of credit issued from loan-offices conducted by the government, and hypothecated upon real or personal security. To this accommodation merchants occasionally had resort when engaged in a venture of peculiar magnitude, but, as a rule, the assistance was unnecessary. Commercial transactions had not yet reached those prodigious proportions to which they have in the present century attained.¹

Gouge's History of Banking and Paper Money, 34. Debates and Proceedings of the General Assembly of Pennsylvania on the Memorials praying a Repeal or Suspension of the Act annulling the Charter of the Bank. Matthew Carey, Editor, Philadelphia, 1786, 37.

As early, however, as the year 1763 the increased business of the port of Philadelphia encouraged some of its principal merchants, among them Robert Morris, to entertain the design of establishing a bank. It was thought by them that such an institution, if conducted upon proper principles, would materially facilitate and increase the American trade. Negotiations were accordingly entered into in Europe with a view to effect this object, and although vigorously opposed by some on the ground that it would give a few men a monopoly of trade, the institution would no doubt have eventually been established had it not been for the breaking out of the War of the Revolution.

1775 An entirely new set of financial problems was

---

¹ South Carolina is indeed said to have established a public bank in the year 1712, from which £48000 in bills of credit were issued, called bank-bills. This institution seems, however, to have been only the ordinary colonial loan-office under another name. 2 Holmes, Am. Ann., 82.

now presented to the American mind. Commerce, it is true, had almost perished. Storehouses were empty, and ships were rotting at the quays. But a national system of finance had become a necessity. A national government was to be supported, and a national army to be raised, paid, fed, and clothed.

The various schemes of Congress to this end were badly planned and worse executed. It had resort to paper money, to lotteries, and to loans both foreign and domestic, but by the close of 1779 had almost come to the end of its resources. Its paper money had already depreciated to below one-eighth of its par value, and was still rapidly on the decline, its lotteries proved so many gigantic bubbles, disappointing alike to the government and the adventurers, and its credit seemed far too much exhausted to hope for further cash loans to any large extent.

From these trying difficulties the genius of Alexander Hamilton conceived that the country might be rescued by a plan similar to that already proposed by Morris for its commercial aggrandizement. With characteristic energy he advised the immediate establishment of a vast banking institution, to be known as "The Company of the Bank of the United States," with a capital of two hundred millions of dollars. He proposed that it should be incorporated by Congress for a term of ten years,

1775

1779

1779

1 Hamilton's Works, 116.

and that its capital should be devoted largely to relieving the government from its mortifying financial embarrassments.

The scheme, however, was of far too vast a character to be put into practical shape. As far as can be ascertained it elicited but meagre attention, and meantime the pecuniary condition of the country went from bad to worse.

1780

Dissertations on Government, the Affairs of the Bank, and Paper Money, by Thos. Paine. Philadelphia, 1786, 17.

The spring of the year 1780 was perhaps the most disastrous period of the American Revolution. The credit of Congress, already stretched to the very uttermost, had almost vanished. The army was in great distress. Lack of food, clothes, and pay engendered frequent and dangerous mutinies. "The measures of government, from the want of money, means, and credit, dragged on like a heavy-loaded carriage without wheels." To crown all, the reliance that had been placed in the defences of Charleston now failed. The effect of its anticipated loss on the spirits of the people was greatly dreaded. Already bitter complaints were being made to Congress of over-taxation. "How the public measures were to be carried on, the country defended, and the army recruited, clothed, fed, and paid . . . was a matter too gloomy to

Ibid., 18.

look at." Many who had before been most confident now declared that they despaired of a successful issue. Indeed, a general apathy and gloom seemed to settle on the national cause.

It was under these distressing circumstances that the first banking institution of the country sprang into being. A number of patriotic gentlemen in Philadelphia, who appreciated and deplored the national distress, resolved that from their private fortunes they would do something for the relief of the government. Prominent among these were Robert Morris, Blair McClenachan, Thomas Willing, John Nixon, James Wilson, George Clymer, William Bingham, and a number of others whose names are associated alike with the history of the State and of the nation.

A meeting of citizens was accordingly called in the Coffee-House on June 8, 1780, which was largely attended, and it was then and there resolved that a subscription should instantly be set on foot "to be given in bounties to promote the recruiting service of the United States." The subscriptions rolled up rapidly. Within nine days there was raised no less a sum than four hundred pounds in hard money and one hundred and one thousand three hundred and sixty pounds in Continental money.

While this subscription was going forward information of the loss of Charleston arrived. A few members of Congress, who had observed the movement with interest, at once communicated to the gentlemen who were at the head of it the increased distress and danger to which the country was now subjected, and urged that their benevolent scheme for the national good should be pressed beyond the limits originally intended. Accordingly, on June 17 another meeting was called of the original subscribers and of such other gentlemen as chose to attend, in the City Tavern, and it was resolved to abandon the original plan. In its place, it was proposed to open a security subscription to the amount of three hundred thousand pounds Pennsylvania currency in real money, the subscribers to execute bonds to the amount of their various subscriptions, and the whole amount to form the capital of a bank, by the aid of which it was proposed to supply and transport food to the army. The plan found ready acceptance. "Whereas, in the present situation of public affairs," ran the heading of the subscription-list, "the greatest and most vigorous exertions are necessary for the successful management of the just and necessary war in which we are engaged with Great Britain, we, the subscribers, deeply impressed with the sentiments that on such an occasion should govern us, in the prosecution of a war on the event of which our own freedom and that of our posterity, and the freedom and independence of the United States, are all involved,— hereby severally pledge our property and credit for the several sums specified and mentioned after our names, in order to support the credit of a bank to be established for furnishing a supply of provisions for the armies of the United States."

Within a few days the subscription-list was completed. It embraced the names of all those who had subscribed to the former undertaking and of many others, ninety-two in all, who pledged themselves for amounts which varied from one to ten thousand pounds.[1]

1780
[2] Hazard's Historical Register, 260.

---

[1] The following is the list of subscribers to the Pennsylvania Bank, together with the various amounts contributed by them:

Joseph Reed	£2,000	Michael Hillegas	£4,000
Robert Morris	10,000	Charles Pettit	2,000
Blair McClenachan	10,000	John Mitchell	2,000
James Wilson	5,000	Matthew Irwin	5,000
George Clymer	5,000	Thomas Irwin	5,000
William Bingham	5,000	John Philip de Haas	5,000
J. M. Nesbitt & Co.	5,000	Philip Moore	5,000
Richard Peters	5,000	Robert Knox	2,000
Samuel Meredith	5,000	Joseph Bullock	2,000
James Mease	5,000	John Nixon	5,000
Thomas Barclay	5,000	Francis Gurney	2,000
Samuel Morris, Jr.	5,000	George Campbell	2,000
John Cox	5,000	William Lewis	2,000
Robert L. Hooper, Jr.	5,000	John Mease	4,000
Hugh Shiell	5,000	John Wharton	2,000
Benjamin G. Eyre	4,000	Benjamin Rush	2,000
William Coats	4,000	T. Lawrence	2,000
Emanuel Eyre	5,000	Joseph Blewer	2,000
John Dunlap	4,000	John Pringle	2,000
James Budden	4,000	Bunner, Murray & Co.	6,000
Cadwalader Morris	2,500	Joseph Carson	4,000
Robert Bass	2,000	Matthew Clarkson	2,000
Owen Biddle	2,000	William Hall	2,000
John Gibson	2,000	John Patton	2,000

1780

An organization was at once effected under the name of the "Pennsylvania Bank." The subscribers agreed to pay in ten per cent. of their subscriptions at once, and the residue from time to time as it should be needed. Robert Morris, John M. Nesbitt, Blair McClenachan, Samuel Miles, and Cadwalader Morris were elected Inspectors; John Nixon and George Clymer, Directors; and Tench Francis, Factor.

2 Hazard's Historical Register, 257.

The directors were authorized to borrow money on the credit of the bank for six months or for

Thomas Leiper	£4,000	John Schaffer	£2,000
Robert Bridges	5,000	Alexander Tod	2,000
B. Fuller	2,000	John Purviance	2,000
B. Randolph	2,000	Kean & Nichols	4,000
Abraham Bickley	2,000	John Wilcocks	2,000
George Meade & Co.	2,000	Samuel Ingles	2,000
John Benezet	5,000	Jonathan Penrose	2,000
John Donaldson	2,000	Nathaniel Falconer	2,000
Henry Hill	5,000	James Caldwell	2,000
John Morgan	5,000	Samuel Caldwell	1,000
John Steinmetz	2,000	Samuel Penrose	1,000
Samuel Miles	3,000	William Turnbull	1,000
Samuel Mifflin	5,000	John Shee	1,000
Thomas Mifflin	5,000	Benjamin Davis	1,000
Andrew Hodge	2,000	Sharp Delany	1,000
Thomas Willing	5,000	Samuel Morris	3,000
Samuel Powel	5,000	Andrew Doz	1,000
Charles Thomson	3,000	Gerardus Clarkson	2,000
Henry Keppele	2,000	Peter Whiteside	1,000
Francis C. Hasenclever	2,000	Andrew Robeson	1,000
Isaac Melcher	2,000	Abraham Shoemaker	2,000
Isaac Moses	3,000	Tench Francis	5,000

less time, and to emit notes bearing interest at the rate of six per cent. They were to apply all money borrowed or received from Congress for the sole purpose of purchasing provisions and rum for the use of the Continental army, to transportation, and to discharging the notes and expenses of the bank. Congress was expected from time to time to reimburse the bank for the amounts expended, and when the whole amount laid out should have been thus returned, the notes were to be paid off and cancelled, the accounts settled, and the bank wound up.

On June 21 Congress was officially advised of the organization of the institution, and that it now lacked only the recognition and co-operation of that body. A committee was at once appointed to confer with the subscribers, and so satisfactory was its report that the following resolutions were at once unanimously agreed to:

Resolved, That Congress entertain a high sense of the liberal offer of the association to raise and transport supplies, and that it accepts the same as a distinguished proof of the patriotism of the subscribers; and

Resolved, That the faith of the United States be pledged to the subscribers for their effectual reimbursement in the premises, that bills of exchange to the amount of £15,000 be deposited with the bank, and that, if it should occasionally need

1780

Journal of Congress, June 21, 1780.

1780

8 Smith's Laws, 386, note.

assistance, Congress will advance as much of the current funds as can be spared from other services.

On July 17 the bank began its operations. It was established on Front Street, two doors above Walnut, and, if we may judge from the advertisements of the time, did a fair share of business.

"All persons who have already lent money," runs the notice in the papers of the day, "are desired to apply for bank-notes, and the Directors request the favor of those who may hereafter lodge their cash in the bank that they would tie it up in bundles of bills of one denomination, with labels, their names indorsed, as the business will thereby be done with less trouble and greater despatch." The bank hours were from nine in the morning until noon, and again from three until five in the afternoon.

For nearly a year and a half the Pennsylvania Bank remained open. The factor drew from time to time on the directors for specie, for Pennsylvania State money, or for Continental money, as he had need. These sums he invested in flour, beef, pork, sugar, coffee, salt, and other goods, which he stored in large quantities, and from time to time forwarded to the army. Three millions of rations were provided in this way, besides three hundred barrels of rum. It was thought that these supplies could not have been obtained but for the assistance of the bank, so that it was universally esteemed as having been of most essential service to the country.

The tenth and last instalment of the subscriptions was called in on November 15, 1780, and the bank's affairs finally wound up towards the close of the year 1784.

1780

2 Hazard's Historical Register, 257.

Pennsylvania Gazette, December 29, 1784.

CHAPTER II.

1781.

Financial Condition of the Country in 1781—Ratification of the Articles of Confederation in March, 1781—Appointment of Robert Morris as Superintendent of Finance in February, 1781—Morris's Plan for a National Bank—Action of Congress in Reference thereto—Reasons for establishing a National Bank—The Subscriptions to the Undertaking—The Organization of the Bank of North America in November, 1781—Thomas Willing elected President—The Ordinance of Incorporation passed by Congress December 31, 1781.

THE year 1781 opened with prospects which were gloomy indeed to contemplate. In January a large part of the American army quartered at Morristown mutinied for lack of pay, declared their intention of departing to their homes, and were only restrained from carrying their threat into execution by the personal influence and solicitation of the commander-in-chief. Congress despaired of raising sufficient supplies. One delegate from Virginia seriously proposed that General Washington should be authorized to lay violent hands upon all the provisions that could be found within twenty miles of his camp. Members of the Board of War declared they had not the means of sending an express from Philadelphia to the army.

Debates and Proceedings of the General Assembly of Pennsylvania on the Memorials praying a Repeal or Suspension of the Law annulling the Charter of the Bank, Matthew Carey, Editor. Philadelphia, 1786, 47.

Continental money had fallen to about one per cent. of its par value, and within four months of the beginning of the year had begun altogether to lose its purchasing power. "The Congress is finally bankrupt," said a Tory paper of May, 1781. "Last night a large body of the inhabitants, with paper dollars in their hats by way of cockades, paraded the streets of Philadelphia, carrying colors flying, with a dog tarred, and, instead of the usual appendage and ornament of feathers, his back was covered with the Congress paper dollars.... This example was directly followed by the jailer, who refused accepting the bills in purchase of a glass of rum, and afterwards by the traders of the city, who shut up their shops, declining to sell any more goods but for gold and silver." 1781

Rivington's Gazette, May 12, 1781.

But as the year went on there was a decided improvement in the complexion of public affairs.

On the 1st of March the Articles of Confederation were finally ratified, and, however imperfect in their structure, certainly established more definite relations than had formerly existed among the States. By them all charges of war, and other expenses incurred for the common defence and safety, were made payable out of a common treasury, and Congress was given express power to borrow money and emit bills of credit, all debts so contracted being deemed a charge against the United States

1781 for the payment of which they and the public faith were pledged.

Journal of Congress, February 20, 1781.

Hardly less important was the election by Congress of Robert Morris as Superintendent of Finance on the 20th of February, 1781. Wearied at last by the endless mistakes and delays of the boards and committees who had had the control of the finances, Congress at last resolved to commit them to the management of a single responsible head. It was universally conceded that they had acted most wisely in preferring Morris to the post. Full of energy and self-reliance, he was, perhaps, by his business talents and mercantile experience, better qualified than any man in America to control and direct its financial affairs. He thought no sacrifice too great to be made for the service of his country. Possessed of a splendid personal credit, he often racked it to the uttermost to carry on some favorite national project. He spared neither labor, time, nor thought, and, whatever strictures may be made on his management of the national treasury, it must be confessed that it was characterized by a consistency and vigor which the country had not before witnessed.

Letter, Alexander Hamilton to Robert Morris, April 30, 1781, 1 Hamilton's Works, 222.

Hamilton took an early occasion to congratulate Morris on his appointment, and at once urged on him the advisability of proposing the establishment of a national bank. This, according to his views, should have a capital of at least three millions of dollars, and be carried on in close relations with the national government.

1781

Morris was the more ready to comply with this suggestion because it coincided to a great degree with his own convictions. He felt persuaded that the establishment of a national bank could not but be of great service both to the government and to commerce, but he was unwilling to embark in an undertaking of such magnitude as had been conceived by the daring mind of Hamilton. He drew up, therefore, a scheme on a scale which he felt to be adequate to the national wants and certain to secure popular approbation, and on the 17th of May, 1781, presented to Congress his plan for the establishment of the Bank of North America.

The details of this plan were sufficiently simple. A subscription of four hundred thousand dollars was to be raised, in shares of four hundred dollars each, payable in gold or silver. Every subscriber of five shares or upwards was to undertake to pay one-half the sum on the day of his subscription and the other half within three months of that date. When the whole sum was made up, a systematic organization was to be effected. Twelve directors were to be chosen annually to regulate the affairs of the bank, none of whom were to receive any compensation for their services except by consent of the stockholders. These were in turn annually to elect one of their number as presi-

1781 dent, and quarterly to elect two of their number as inspectors, to control the affairs of the bank. The shares were to be freely transferable, and the directors were to be at liberty to open new subscriptions to the capital stock as often and upon such terms as they should see proper. The bank was to be distinctively a national institution. On every evening, Sunday excepted, the inspectors were to deliver to the Superintendent of Finance an accurate account of the day's business, and it was understood that at all times he should have full right to examine into its affairs. Its bank-notes, payable on demand, were by law to be made receivable for duties and taxes in every State in the Union, and were to be deemed in the settlement of accounts between the States and the United States as specie. Other regulations were to be made relating to the conduct of its affairs, which, being of minor importance, need not here be recapitulated.

Journal of Congress, May 17, 1781.

The matter was deemed by Congress of great importance, and was at once referred to a special committee of four, with instructions to report on the feasibility of the scheme. This committee consisted of Witherspoon of New Jersey, Sullivan of New Hampshire, M. Smith of Virginia, and Clymer of Pennsylvania. On May 26 it reported in favor of the adoption of the plan. Resolutions were at once introduced in consonance with its recommendations, and a lively debate ensued. The promoters of the bank used every argument which a thorough belief in its usefulness could inspire. Madison, on the contrary, was bitterly opposed. He contended that Congress was quite overstepping its powers in pledging itself to establish a banking institution, and there were others who coincided with him in opinion.

When at length the vote was taken the resolutions were found to have been passed by a bare majority only. New Hampshire, New Jersey, Maryland, Virginia, North Carolina, South Carolina, and Georgia voted aye. Rhode Island and Connecticut were insufficiently represented. Pennsylvania was divided, Mr. T. Smith voting no and Mr. Clymer voting aye. Massachusetts alone was registered in the negative.

The following are the resolutions in question:

Resolved, That Congress do approve of the plan for establishing a national bank in these United States, submitted by Mr. Robert Morris the 17th May, 1781, and that they will promote and support the same by such ways and means from time to time as may appear necessary for the institution and consistent with the public good.

Resolved, That the subscribers to the said bank shall be incorporated agreeably to the principles and terms of the plan, under the name of the President, Directors, and Company of the Bank of North America, so soon as the subscription

1781

6 Bancroft's History of the United States (Centennial Edition), 468.

1781

shall be filled, the directors and president chosen, and application made to Congress for that purpose by the president and directors elected.

Resolved, That it be recommended to the several States, by proper laws for that purpose, to provide that no other Bank or Bankers shall be established or permitted within the said States respectively during the war.

Resolved, That the notes hereafter to be issued by the said bank, payable on demand, shall be receivable in payment of all taxes, duties, and debts due, or that may become due and payable to the United States.

Resolved, That Congress will recommend to the several Legislatures to pass laws making it felony without benefit of clergy, for any person to counterfeit bank-notes, or to pass such notes, knowing them to be counterfeited; also making it felony without benefit of clergy, for any president, inspector, director, officer, or servant of the bank to convert any of the property, money, or credit of the said bank to his own use, or in any other way to be guilty of fraud or embezzlement, as officers or servants of the bank.

Journal of Congress, May 26, 1781.

The plan being approved by Congress, the Superintendent of Finance, on May 28, published it to the world, accompanied by an address, in which he set forth the necessity and prudence of the measure. "To ask," said he, "the end which it is proposed to answer by this institution of a bank, is merely to call the public attention to the situation of our affairs. A depreciating paper currency has unhappily been the source of infinite private mischief, numberless frauds, and the greatest distress. The national calamities have moved with an equal pace, and the public credit has received the deepest injury. This is a circumstance so unusual in a republican government that we may boldly affirm it cannot continue a moment after the several Legislatures have determined to take those vigorous and effectual measures to which the public voice now loudly commands their attention. In the mean time the exigencies of the United States require an anticipation of our revenue; while, at the same time, there is not such confidence established as will call out, for that purpose, the funds of individual citizens. The use, then, of a bank is to aid the government by their moneys and credit, for which they will have every proper reward and security, to gain from individuals that credit which property, abilities, and integrity never failed to command, to supply the loss of that paper money which, becoming more and more useless, calls every day more loudly for its final redemption, and to give a new spring to commerce, in the moment when, on the removal of all its restrictions, the citizens of America shall enjoy and possess that freedom for which they contend."

1781

Facts Respecting the Bank of North America, 4.

Letter, Greene to Morris, August 18, 1781. Greene's Life of Greene, vol. iii. p. 370.

Facts Respecting the Bank of North America, 7.

Belles' Financial History of the United States, 273.

Dissertations on Government, the Affairs of the Bank and Paper Money, by Thos. Paine. Philadelphia, 1786, 20.

The subscriptions meanwhile mounted up slowly. Morris sought, but for the most part in vain, to interest the citizens of other States in the enterprise. In the South particularly he made strenuous efforts, but few were found willing to embark in the undertaking. "The prospect of profit was very remote, the danger of a total loss of capital evident. The country was engaged in an arduous and doubtful conflict. If unsuccessful, the whole capital was lost."

Another serious disappointment about this time occurred to the Superintendent of Finance. He had, in establishing the bank, relied largely for a supply of coin upon the Governor-General of Havana, who was to have been repaid by annual shipments of flour, guaranteed by the French Crown. This negotiation, unfortunately, at the critical moment broke down, and Morris found himself unable to render the bank the expected aid.

In spite of all difficulties, however, the subscription-list began, by the fall of 1781, to present a very respectable appearance. The gentlemen who had been most prominent in the organization of the Pennsylvania Bank became identified at once with the fortunes of the new institution. They readily perceived that, if successful, it would render useless the continuance of the old undertaking. They resolved, therefore, at once to wind up the latter's affairs, and in many instances transferred their subscriptions from its books into those of the Bank of North America.

Other citizens of Philadelphia and its neighborhood, and a few of other parts of the country, came forward, and by October or November it was found that there had been paid in cash about $70,000. About this time a French frigate arrived in Boston, bringing to the national treasury a most opportune remittance of about $470,000 in specie. This sum was immediately brought to Philadelphia and lodged in the vaults of the bank; and so assured did the stockholders now feel of ultimate success in their undertaking that they resolved at once to take steps for organization.

On November 1, 1781, a meeting was convened at the City Tavern.[1] A number of the same

1781

Considerations on the Bank of North America. Philadelphia, 1785, 5.

Debates and Proceedings of the General Assembly of Pennsylvania on the Memorials praying a Repeal or Suspension of the Law annulling the Charter of the Bank. Matthew Carey, Editor. Philadelphia, 1786, 48.

---

[1] At this meeting the following persons were present:

Gouv'r Morris,	James Wilson.
James Crawford.	John Nixon.
Chas. Pettit.	*Timothy Matlack.*
Michael Hillegas.	Andr. & James Caldwell.
Samuel Osgood.	Robt. Morris.
B. Fuller.	Francis Gurney.
Samuel Meredith,	Geo. Meade & Co.
for George Clymer.	Thos. Fitzsimons.
Wm. Turnbull.	Thos. Fitzsimons,
John Wilcocks.	for Geo. Meade.
Jno. Mitchell.	George Haynes.
Samuel Meredith.	David H. Conyngham.
Mease & Caldwell.	J. Ross.
John Donaldson.	

Of these, all but nine, indicated by italics, were subscribers to the Pennsylvania Bank.

Directors' Minutes, November 2, 1781.

1781

Directors' Minutes, November 2, 1781.

Directors' Minutes, November 26, 1781.

Lives of Eminent Philadelphians now Deceased. Tit. "Thomas Willing."

gentlemen who had controlled the affairs of the Pennsylvania Bank were called upon to assume the management of the new national enterprise. The following was the board of directors chosen: Thomas Willing, Thomas Fitzsimons, John Maxwell Nesbitt, James Wilson, Henry Hill, Samuel Osgood, Cadwalader Morris, Andrew Caldwell, Samuel Ingles, Samuel Meredith, William Bingham, and Timothy Matlack. At a meeting of the board held the following day Thomas Willing was elected as president, and, a few days after, Tench Francis as cashier.

Mr. Willing was, from his social position, business talents, and political experience, well qualified to fill the responsible position to which he was now called. He was to be reckoned, undoubtedly, as a leading man in the State, if not in the country at large. Born on the 19th of December, 1731, he was now, at the age of fifty, in the very prime of his powers. He was a partner of Robert Morris in a large and prosperous business, and had served successively as Secretary to the Congress of Delegates at Albany, Judge of the Supreme Court of Pennsylvania, Mayor of Philadelphia, Member of the Colonial Assembly, and President of the Provincial Congress. He was afterwards chosen as a delegate to Congress under the Confederation and as first president of the Bank of the United States.

"His character," says Mr. Binney, "was not

Thos. Willing

PRESIDENT OF THE BANK OF NORTH AMERICA
1782—1791

unlike that of Washington, and, in the discretion of his conduct, the fidelity of his professions, and the great influence, both public and private, which belonged to him, the destined leader (Washington) was certain to find the elements of an affinity by which they would be united in the closest manner." "This excellent man," he says again, "in all the relations of private life, and in various stations of high public trust, deserved and acquired the devoted affection of his family and friends, and the universal respect of his fellow-citizens."

After this happy choice the affairs of the bank rapidly progressed. By December $85,000 in cash had been raised, exclusive of the amount of the government deposit, and, although the subscription was far from complete, it was resolved to apply to Congress for a charter of incorporation. The measure was introduced, but was not passed without some opposition. The opinion had come to be largely entertained that the Confederation contained no power to incorporate a bank. Congress, however, had already pledged its word. Some concessions were made to the scruples of the opposition, and on December 31, 1781, an ordinance was finally passed perpetually incorporating the subscribers by the name and style of "The President, Directors, and Company of the Bank of North America." This ordinance distinctly recognized the fact that the exigencies of

1781

The Republican Court, 161.

Inscription upon his tombstone, written by Horace Binney, Esq.

G. Bancroft's History of the United States (Centennial Edition), 463.

1781 the United States rendered it indispensably necessary that such an institution should be called into being; it conferred the ordinary corporate powers, among them the right to hold property to the value of ten millions of dollars; it recognized the officers already chosen as duly and properly elected, and declared that everything therein contained should "be construed and taken most favorably and beneficially for the said corporation."

A clause was introduced forbidding the bank to exercise any powers in any of the States repugnant to the laws thereof, a provision with which the opponents of the measure declared themselves well satisfied. As a further concession to their prejudices, it was agreed that a supplementary resolution should be passed recommending to the several States to give full force and effect to the incorporating ordinance. This was peculiarly agreeable to Madison, who regarded the requisition as a tacit admission by Congress of their defect of power.

Journal of Congress, December 31, 1781.

CHAPTER III.

1782-1784.

The Bank of North America begins its Operations on January 7, 1782—Circular Letter of the Superintendent of Finance announcing this Fact to the Governors of the various States—Early Difficulties experienced by the Bank—Stories relating to it circulated by its Enemies—Rapid Success of the Institution—Recognition of its Existence by Connecticut, Rhode Island, and Massachusetts in January and March, 1782—A Charter granted to it by the Assembly of Pennsylvania on March 26, 1782—Opposition to Mr. Willing on Account of alleged Disloyalty—Assistance afforded by the Bank to the National Government—Assistance afforded by it to the State of Pennsylvania—Assistance afforded by it to the City of Philadelphia—Proposed Establishment of the Bank of Pennsylvania in 1784—Abandonment of the Scheme in Consequence of the Increase in the Capital Stock of the Bank of North America—Subscriptions to the New Stock.

ON the 7th of January, 1782, the Bank of North America began active operations. Its business was conducted in a commodious store belonging to its cashier, Tench Francis, situate on the north side of Chestnut Street, a short distance west of Third, which had previously been leased and fitted up for its accommodation.[1] In these

<small>Considerations on the Bank of North America. Philadelphia, 1785, 29.

Directors' Minutes, November 20, 1781.</small>

---

[1] The bank subsequently purchased the lot and buildings thereon. The following is an abstract of the title:

1782 quarters the bank continued its operations for upwards of sixty-five years.[1]

Tench Francis *et ux* to John Wilson, May 24, 1792. (See Deed Book, No. 36, page 105, etc.)

John Wilson *et ux* to Mordecai Lewis, Miers Fisher, and Robert Waln, as Trustees for the Bank, December 20, 1793. (See Deed Book, No. 40, page 522, etc.)

Robert Waln, surviving Trustee, *et ux* to The President, Directors, and Company of the Bank of North America, February 3, 1821. (See Deed Book F. W., No. 9, page 198, etc.)

[1] The following is a description of the Banking House as it appeared on December 3, 1839, taken from a survey made that day by the surveyor of the "Philadelphia Contributionship":

"The Bank of North America, situate on the north side of Chesnut Street, west of and near Third Street, being 38 feet front by 45 feet deep, three stories high, exclusive of an octagon back, one story high, 18 and 9 inch walls. The lower story is one main room, with three small apartments, divided off by a boarding about four feet high, with turned ballusters on the top, for the use of the President, Cashier, and a discount-room, and a counter in the middle nearly the length of the main room; a girder under the second floor supported by three turn'd columns; a large vault on the west side of the room three stories high, with iron doors opening into it in each story, and a small fire-proof in two of the small rooms above mentioned; . . . single architraves and mouldings to the windows; a vestibule inside the front door, with folding sash-doors hung in it; glass, 13 by 19 inches; outside shutters front and back; two plain marble mantels in the lower story.

"The second story is divided into four rooms and passage; . . . base and surbase round; double and single architraves to the doors and windows; two marble mantels, with open pilasters; recess closets; glass, 13 by 19 inches, pannel'd inside; shutters front and back and outside do. to the back windows.

"The third story in four rooms and passage, . . . plain base and surbase round; single architraves and mouldings; glass, in front, 13 by 27 inches; back, 9 by 11; plain stairs, with windows in the lower

The bank hours were from ten in the morning until one in the afternoon, and again from three in the afternoon until five.

1782
Directors' Minutes, November 5, 1782.

The regular employés of the bank were only six in number,—the cashier, the teller, the sub-teller, the accomptant, the clerk, and the porter. They received very inconsiderable salaries,—the cashier but $1000 a year, the porter but $160. The accounts were all kept in Mexican dollars and ninetieth parts thereof. Directors' meetings were held every Thursday, and two members of the board were chosen monthly to inspect and control the affairs of the bank.

The institution being now fairly under way, the Superintendent of Finance issued the following circular letter announcing the fact to the governors of the various States:

OFFICE OF FINANCE, January 8th, 1782.

SIR,—I have the honor to transmit herewith an ordinance passed by the United States, in Congress assembled, the thirty-first day of December, 1781, incorporating the subscribers to the Bank of North America, together with sundry resolutions, recommending to the several States to pass such Laws as they may judge necessary for giving the said ordinance its full operation. The reso-

corner leading from the lower to the third story; garret plastered, and plain sky-light in the roof.

"Old-fashioned wooden eaves; the front dentil, lack plain; roof covered with copper, and copper pipes down; the cellar floored with brick, and two furnaces therein, which appear to be safely constructed."

1782 lutions of the 26th May last speak so clearly to the points necessary to be established by these Laws, that I need not enlarge on them. Should anything more be found necessary upon experience, the President and Directors will, no doubt, make suitable application to Congress, or to the States respectively, as the case may require. It affords me great satisfaction to inform your Excellency that this Bank commenced its operations yesterday, and I am confident that, with proper management, it will answer the most sanguine expectations of those who befriend the Institution. It will facilitate the management of the Finances of the United States. The several States may, when their respective necessities require, and the abilities of the Bank will permit, derive occasional advantage and accommodation from it. It will afford to the individuals of all the States a medium for their intercourse with each other and for the payment of Taxes, more convenient than the precious metals, and equally safe. It will have a tendency to increase both the internal and external Commerce of North America, and, undoubtedly, will be infinitely useful to all the Traders of every State in the Union, provided, as I have already said, it is conducted on the principles of equity, justice, prudence, and economy. The present Directors bear characters that cannot fail to inspire confidence, and, as the corporation is amenable to the Laws, power can neither sanctify any improper conduct nor protect the guilty. Under a full conviction of these things, I flatter myself that I shall stand excused for recommending in the strongest manner this well-meant plan to all the encouragement and protection which your State can give consistently with Wisdom and Justice.

  I have the honor to be, with great respect,

    Your Excellency's most obedient &

        Most h'ble serv't,

          Rob't Morris.

9 Pennsylvania Archives, 477.

The first operations of the bank were attended with considerable difficulty. Morris, in order to strengthen its position as far as possible, subscribed, on account of the United States, what remained of the specie lately arrived from France. With the utmost care and caution he had only been able to retain about $254,000 of this sum, and this amount enabled him to buy in for the national treasury 633 shares of bank stock. But what he thus paid in with one hand he may be said to have drawn out with the other. Within a very short period the great necessities of the country obliged him to borrow from the bank amounts far exceeding the sum subscribed, so that the institution had little benefit from it as a means of establishing its credit. Nor was the whole amount of the individual subscriptions yet paid in, owing to the great scarcity of money. As a consequence, the amount of specie in the vaults at times dwindled to an alarming extent, and so great were the fears of an early exhaustion of this sum, that at critical periods men were regularly employed to follow those who demanded specie and urge them to return it in order to preserve the precious foundation.

In addition to all this, it was found that the notes of the bank would not readily circulate. Army contractors, when paid in this way, almost invariably carried the bills to collectors, and got

1782

Debates and Proceedings of the General Assembly of Pennsylvania on the Memorials praying a Repeal or Suspension of the Law annulling the Charter of the Bank. Matthew Carey, Editor. Philadelphia, 1786, 48.

Official Accounts of the United States from 1781 to 1784.

Bolles' Financial History of the United States, 273.

the amount in specie. In New England, the people, fresh from the recollection of Continental money, were very loath to receive the bank issues at all, so that they circulated at from ten to fifteen per cent. below par. Stories were current, and actually believed, that the bank made a show of far greater wealth than it actually possessed. "Gentlemen interested in the institution," it was said, "were in the habit of requesting people from the country and laboring men about town to go to the bank and get silver in exchange for notes. When they went on this errand of neighborly kindness, as they thought it, they found a display of silver on the counter, and men employed in raising boxes containing silver, or supposed to contain silver, from the cellar to the banking-room, or lowering them from the banking-room into the cellar," by which contrivances they were induced to believe that the bank was possessed of immense wealth.

But all difficulties were soon overcome. A considerable sum in specie arrived from Europe and the West Indies, and little by little the amounts subscribed by individuals to the capital stock were paid into the treasury. The deposits gradually rolled up. Morris, by skilful management, prevented further issues from floating into that part of the country where they were badly received. The depreciation was quickly checked. Bank-

Margin notes:
1782
Letter, Alexander Hamilton to Robert Morris, September 21, 1782. Hamilton's Works, vol. i. p. 308.
Bolles' Financial History of the United States, 273.
Gouge's History of Paper Money and Banking, 35.

THE BANK OF NORTH AMERICA. 43

bills rose to their par value, and were there sustained without further trouble. The directors felt every reason for encouragement, a general confidence succeeded to the former mistrust, and by November the stockholders were able to congratulate the officers upon "the skill and attention they had manifested in arranging an institution altogether new in America, the good effects of which," they declared, "the public had already experienced."

Meantime, in spite of the early difficulties of the bank, some of the States had not been backward in acknowledging its existence.

On January 10 the Assembly of Connecticut passed an act declaring that the bank's notes should be receivable in payment of all taxes due the State. About the same time the Assembly of Rhode Island passed a law for the punishment of those who might counterfeit its notes or embezzle its funds, and on March 8 the State of Massachusetts actually created it a corporation according to the laws of that Commonwealth.

Much doubt being entertained as to the validity of the charter granted by Congress, it was now thought by the Board of Directors that the credit and efficiency of the organization might be materially assisted if a charter could be obtained from the State of Pennsylvania.

A memorial to that effect was drawn up, and on

1782

Bolles' Financial History of the United States, 274.

Stockholders' Minutes, November 4, 1782.

Considerations on the Bank of North America, 6.

1782

February 9 transmitted, with the following letter, to the President of the Supreme Executive Council:

> SIR,—The President, Directors, and Company of the Bank of North America, incorporated by the United States, in Congress assembled, have thought it proper to petition the General Assembly for a similar charter, and such support from the government of the State, as may render the bank capable of yielding those advantages to the general cause of America which are intended thereby; and this institution being encouraged and supported by citizens of other States, as well as that in which it happens to be established, the most respectful and proper mode of presenting the petition to the Honorable House appearing to be through the Supreme Executive Council of the State, we have inclosed the same to you, and request you to lay it before the General Assembly as soon as they shall meet. I have the honor to be
>
> Your Excellency's most obedient servant,
>
> THOMAS WILLING, President.
>
> His Excellency WILLIAM MOORE, ESQ., President.

Considerations on the Bank of North America, 32.

Journal of Assembly, February 21, 1782.

Journal of Assembly, February 25, 1782.

On February 21 President Moore forwarded the memorial to the Assembly, and on the 25th a bill was introduced providing for the incorporation of the bank. Its terms were in every respect identical with those of the ordinance of Congress already mentioned. On the 25th of the ensuing March the bill had reached its final stages without serious opposition, but at this point difficulties arose. The attribute of perpetual existence, and the capacity to hold a large amount of property, both of which were conferred by the proposed charter, seemed, in the eyes of some members, dangerous to the true interests of the State. It was, therefore, proposed that a clause should be inserted limiting the period of the bank's existence to seven years, and prohibiting it from holding real estate. These proposed amendments were readily rejected, but on the following day still another difficulty was found to stand in the way. An opinion was entertained by some of the members of the Assembly that the president of the bank, Mr. Willing, had not at one period manifested sufficient zeal in the national cause.

1782

Journal of Assembly, March 25, 1782.

Ibid., March 26, 1782.

While the British were in possession of Philadelphia in 1777, Sir William Howe despatched from time to time messengers charged with secret offers to the various members of Congress, with the hope of inducing them to conclude a peace on some other basis than that of independence. Among those who were thus sent out was one John Brown, who had the misfortune to be arrested by the American troops, and was by resolution of Congress brought before the Pennsylvania Council of Safety. Upon his examination before that body he declared that he had been induced to embark in the undertaking chiefly through the solicitations of Mr. Willing. This story now afforded ground to some of the bitter Whigs in the House to refuse their assent to the confirmation of Mr. Willing in his office. They wished to have

Minutes of the Council of Safety, November 21 and 22, 1777. 11 Colonial Records, 344, 347.

1782 the whole clause nominating the officers stricken out, and accordingly made a motion to that effect. "We consider it," said they, "highly impolitic and unjust to recognize and establish by an act of the Legislature in so eminent and honorable a station the man who not only abandoned the cause of our country in the hour of our deepest distress and calamity, but whilst the British army was in Philadelphia actually suffered himself to be employed by them as the instrument and agent of their insidious attempts to debauch the minds of the people, and even to reduce our public councils into submission. We think that loading with honors a man who so lately did what he could to enslave this country is a discouragement to the Whigs, is a wound to the cause of patriotism, and is trampling on the blood of those heroes and martyrs who have fallen in defence of our liberty."

<small>Journal of Assembly, March 26, 1782.</small>

Notwithstanding all opposition, the bill at length passed in its original shape. A desperate effort was subsequently made to reserve to the Assembly, in 1789, a right to withdraw the privileges they had conferred, but the attempt failed. The bank accepted the new charter, and continued its operations as an institution duly incorporated under the laws of Pennsylvania.

<small>Ibid., April 1, 1782.</small>

The advantages derived from the establishment of the bank soon answered the most sanguine expectations of its projector. In a wonderfully short time it restored confidence and credit, at least in some degree, to the commercial world. Nor was the assistance which it was enabled to afford the Government less valuable. In the beginning of the year 1782 the United States owed considerable sums of money. The requisitions made by Congress for the expenses of the coming year amounted to eight millions of dollars. But the States were not called on to pay this sum until the 1st of April, and, as a matter of fact, the requisitions produced so little effect that by the end of June not more than $30,000 had been raised. "At that period," says the Superintendent of Finance, "the public credit had gone to wreck, and the enemy built their most sanguine hopes of overcoming us upon this circumstance, but at this crisis our credit was restored by the bank."

The aid afforded to the Government by actual cash advances was alone very considerable. During January, February, and March of 1782 the bank loaned for this purpose, in all, the sum of $300,000. By July 1 $100,000 more had been advanced, making a total of $400,000 during the year. Nor was this the only advantage reaped by the United States Treasury. Holding as it did at this period $253,000$\frac{23}{90}$ in bank stock, or rather more than five-eighths of the whole capital of the institution, it received, in common with the other stockholders,

1782

Debates and Proceedings of the General Assembly of Pennsylvania on the Memorials praying a Repeal or Suspension of the Law annulling the Charter of the Bank. Matthew Carey, Editor. Philadelphia, 1786, 49.

Ibid.
Statement of the Accounts of the United States, 1782-1784.

the very large dividends which were declared by the bank, much more than compensating for the interest which it paid upon its loans.

In December the president and directors grew uneasy at the extent of the Government loan, and asked for some reduction. The Superintendent of Finance accordingly sold out $200,000 of the Government stock, and paid to the bank $300,000 of the amount borrowed. During the first half of the year 1783 the bank advanced to the Government about $30,000. In July the rest of the Government stock was sold, principally to capitalists in Holland. By October 1 $25,000 more had been advanced to the national treasury, making the aggregate advance at that time about $165,000. This amount was not finally paid off until January 1, 1784.

In addition to the actual cash advances made to the Government, the bank was enabled in several other ways to afford it invaluable assistance. The large amount of specie deposited in the bank vaults enabled it from time to time to discount in considerable amounts bills drawn on the Superintendent of Finance, so that the public agents were enabled to purchase for cash, and the Treasury was afforded time to provide the means of payment. It was in this way that the army was supplied with clothes and provisions, and the various public departments largely assisted until the close of the war. Before

Sidenotes:

1782

Montefiore's Dictionary of Commerce, American Edition, 1803. Tit. "Bank of North America."

Debates and Proceedings of the General Assembly of Pennsylvania on the Memorials praying a Repeal or Suspension of the Law annulling the Charter of the Bank. Matthew Carey, Editor. Philadelphia, 1786, 4°.

Statement of the Accounts of the United States, 1782–1784.

July 1, 1783, discounts of this kind had been made to the extent of $820,000. "Without the establishment of the national bank," said Morris, "the business of the Department of Finance could not have been performed. From the aids given by this institution the United States were able to keep up an army consisting of a larger number of men than they had had in the field before, or than they could have maintained without these aids. The army was in every point on a much more respectable footing than formerly, and they kept the enemy at bay."

"But the United States were not the only persons benefited by this institution. The Legislature of the State of Pennsylvania, being unable to pay the officers of their army, granted them certificates of indebtedness, and mortgaged the revenue of the excise for payment of interest. When the interest became due the revenue was not collected, and the distress of the officers was great. On that occasion, without any particular application, the bank advanced the money, and took the reimbursement when the revenue was collected."

Again, in February, 1782, when the State of Pennsylvania found itself so embarrassed that it was unable to pay its quota to the United States Government, the bank, without hesitation, agreed to advance $80,000 on its behalf.

During the first few months of the same year,

1782

Debates and Proceedings of the General Assembly of Pennsylvania on the Memorials praying a Repeal or Suspension of the Law annulling the Charter of the Bank. Matthew Carey, Editor. Philadelphia. 1786, 49.

Ibid., 50.

Ibid., 105.

1782

Debates and Proceedings of the General Assembly of Pennsylvania on the Memorials praying a Repeal or Suspension of the Law annulling the Charter of the Bank. Matthew Carey, Editor. Philadelphia, 1786, 106.

when, owing to the unprotected state of Delaware Bay and River, the enemy's row-boats sometimes took vessels within the very Port of Philadelphia, and the State had not the means of granting protection against so inconsiderable though insulting an enemy, the bank, by an advance of about $22,500, enabled the merchants to fit out a ship, which, within a few days, not only cleared the Bay and River, but captured a cruiser of twenty guns belonging to the British fleet.

On September 17, 1782, the bank advanced to the State Treasurer, for the defence of the western frontiers, no less than £5000, and even agreed to lend a further sum if necessity should arise. In January, 1785, it loaned the City Wardens $2400, and the Managers of the House of Employment $4000. In short, it proved of most material assistance both in State and municipal affairs. "The instances of its services," said a distinguished mercantile gentleman of the time, "are innumerable. Ask the managers of the House of Employment. They will tell you the poor could not have been fed without the existence of the bank. Ask the wardens of the city, and they will tell you that the city could not have been lighted but by means of the loans obtained there. But it is needless to repeat the instances, for I may say there is no service, public or charitable, to which its assistance has been denied."

Ibid.

By the beginning of the year 1784 the success of the bank was assured. The business and the profits alike rapidly increased, so that, notwithstanding the heavy loans with which they obliged the public, the directors were enabled to declare annual dividends for that and the following year at an average rate of fourteen per cent., thus making bank stock the most desirable of investments.

So great, indeed, was the demand made upon the bank for loans to aid both public and private enterprises, that the stockholders now felt emboldened to increase the amount of their capital. On January 12, 1784, they accordingly authorized the directors to open the books of the bank on the 1st of the following February for a new subscription of one thousand shares, at the rate of $500 a share, the new stockholders to stand on a par with the old, and to pay the amount of their various subscriptions at once. The shares were rapidly taken up, but meantime a difficulty arose which had not been anticipated.

A number of influential citizens, who saw and envied the success of the Bank of North America, were anxious to participate in the profits of so lucrative a business, but did not feel disposed to pay the difference between the original and the advanced value of its shares. They resolved, therefore, to set on foot a rival institution, to be known by the name of the Bank of Pennsylvania.

1784

Debates and Proceedings of the General Assembly of Pennsylvania on the Memorials praying a Repeal or Suspension of the Law annulling the Charter of the Bank. Matthew Carey, Editor. Philadelphia. 1786, 106.

1784

Political Essays, by Pelatiah Webster, 448.

Journal of Assembly, February 10, 1784.

Ibid., February 26, 1784.

Ibid., February 28, 1784.

Ibid., March 10, 1784.

The directors of the old bank, they assured the public, had been guilty of a haughtiness and partiality in their method of conducting business of which no one would ever find cause to accuse the officers of the new institution. It was better, at any rate, they argued, to have "two shops to go to" in banking as in other business.

Large subscriptions were rapidly got together, and an organization effected. On the 10th of February application was made to the Assembly for a charter. The matter was referred to a committee, who reported in favor of granting the prayer of the memorial. On the 26th the Bank of North America presented an application asking that it might be heard by counsel as to the impropriety of granting the new charter. But no attention was paid to the request, and, on the 28th, the matter was referred to a committee to bring in the draft of a bill. On March 10 the committee reported, and for a while the measure was allowed to lie on the table.

Meantime, the directors and stockholders of the old bank had been looking with great anxiety at the progress of the new enterprise. They strongly urged what to them seemed the fatal consequences of two capital banks operating in one city. They might, they feared, act in opposition to each other, and would be sure eventually to be of mutual disadvantage.

A meeting of the stockholders of the Bank of North America was therefore convened on the 1st of March, and, as an effectual check to the new undertaking, it was resolved to extend the new subscriptions, opened on February 1, to four thousand shares, at the rate of but $400 a share. All those who had already paid in their money at the rate of $500 a share were to have the surplus returned to them, together with interest at the current rate. The device acted admirably. The subscribers to the Bank of Pennsylvania were readily prevailed upon to relinquish their scheme, and to substitute for the uncertain fortunes of a new undertaking a share in the profits of an institution whose success was already assured. On March 16, when the matter came up before the Assembly, the directors of the new bank asked leave to withdraw their application for a charter. Permission to that effect was granted. The subscriptions to the old bank rapidly flowed in, and by June 13, on which date the books were closed, the capital was found to amount to $830,000.

1784

Stockholders' Minutes, March 1, 1784.

Political Essays, by Pelatiah Webster, 448.

4 Hazard's Historical Register, 156.

CHAPTER IV.

1785-1788.

Pennsylvania Paper Currency—Popular Demand for the issuing thereof in 1785—Attitude of the Bank of North America adverse to the Scheme—Growing Unpopularity of the Bank—Petitions presented to the Assembly praying for a Repeal of its Charter—Arguments for and against the Bank—The State Charter annulled on September 13, 1785—Views of the Directors as to this Action—Continuance of the Bank's Operations—A Charter granted to the Bank by the State of Delaware on February 2, 1786—Attempts to obtain a Repeal of the Annulling Act—A New Charter granted by the State of Pennsylvania on March 17, 1787—Provisions of the Charter—Prosperity of the Institution—Establishment of other Banks.

1785   No sooner was the difficulty about the proposed Bank of Pennsylvania settled than another and still fiercer contest was forced upon the Bank of North America. Pennsylvania had before the Revolution been more successful than any other colony in circulating and sustaining the credit of its paper money. The bills had been issued in the shape of loans to individuals, secured by mortgage on their lands, and were payable at the expiration of ten years from the date of emission, a tenth part being usually annually discharged with interest.

THE BANK OF NORTH AMERICA.

By these prudent measures they were, as a rule, kept at par with specie, and never suffered any but slight fluctuations.

A numerous party now arose in the State, who demanded and obtained a renewal of this line of policy. But they readily saw that unless the bank would give the new bills currency the State could never hope to get them into circulation. This the directors were at first both unwilling and unable, to any great extent, to accomplish. Hence the bank came to be regarded by many as the opponent of the paper money scheme. It was in vain that Morris argued that the bank had withdrawn its opposition to the scheme, and showed by the ledgers and accounts the large amounts of the new currency which the bank did actually accept. By March of 1786 it had received on deposit £107,280 14s., or nearly the whole of the emission, except that which had been reserved for the operations of the loan-office. But its early inimical attitude had proved fatal to its popularity.

One source of trouble led to another. The financial distresses of the mercantile world were still undoubtedly great. The total prostration of business during the period of the Revolutionary War had been succeeded, on the conclusion of peace, by an excess of British importations, draining specie from the American market. As a re-

1785

Bolles' Financial History of the United States, 27.

Ibid., 345.

Debates and Proceedings of the General Assembly of Pennsylvania on the Memorials praying a Repeal or Suspension of the Law annulling the Charter of the Bank. Matthew Carey, Editor. Philadelphia, 1786, 119.

1785 sult, money was scarce and usury common. The suffering to which all classes were subjected was great. The public sought some adequate cause for their miseries, and thought they found it in the establishment of the bank. The Democratic party, then just coming into existence and power, embraced the popular opinion. It was not long before the opposition took a tangible shape. On March 21, 1785, a petition was presented to the Assembly, from a number of the inhabitants of Chester County, praying that steps might be taken to repeal the charter of the bank. There was no evil from which the country was suffering but was, in the opinion of the petitioners, to be ascribed to the baleful influences of that institution. Usury, extortion, favoritism, harshness to its creditors, opposition to the favorite schemes of the Assembly, the possession of undue and dangerous political and commercial influence, all these were laid at its doors. The abolition of so harmful an organization they thought was alone necessary for a restoration of public and private prosperity.[1]

Journal of Assembly, March 21, 1785.

[1] "Petitions from a considerable number of the inhabitants of Chester County were read, representing that the bank established at Philadelphia has fatal effects upon the community; that whilst men are enabled by means of the bank to receive near three times the rate of common interest, and at the same time to receive their money at very short warning whenever they have occasion for it, it will be impossible for the husbandman or mechanic to borrow on the former terms of legal interest and distant payments of the principal; that the best

A great number of similar petitions was about the same time presented, and on March 23 a committee was accordingly appointed "to inquire whether the bank established at Philadelphia was compatible with the public safety and that equality which ought ever to prevail between the individuals of a republic."

The controversy once aroused, a war of pamphlets and arguments ensued. The opponents of the bank abounded with objections to its method of transacting business, and urged with vehemence what they deemed its disastrous effects on the community. It enabled men to trade to their own

1785

security will not enable the person to borrow; that experience clearly demonstrates the mischievous consequences of the institution to the fair trader; that impostors have been enabled to support themselves in a fictitious credit by means of a temporary punctuality at the bank, until they have drawn in their honest neighbors to trust them with their property, or to pledge their credit as sureties, and have been finally involved in ruin and distress; that they have repeatedly seen the stopping of discounts at the bank operate on the trading part of the community with a degree of violence scarcely inferior to that of a stagnation of the blood in the human body, hurrying the wretched merchant who hath debts to pay into the hands of griping usurers; that the directors of the bank may give such preference in trade, by advances in money to their particular favorites, as to destroy that equality which ought to prevail in a commercial country; that paper money has often proved beneficial to the State, but the bank forbids it, and the people must acquiesce; therefore, and in order to restore public confidence and private security, they pray that a bill may be brought in, and passed into a law, for repealing the law for incorporating the bank." Journal of the Assembly of Pennsylvania, vol. ix. p. 232, etc.

1785

Considerations on the Bank of North America. Philadelphia, 1785.

Address to the Assembly of Pennsylvania on the Abolition of the Bank of North America. Philadelphia, 1785.

Debates and Proceedings of the General Assembly of Pennsylvania on the Memorials praying a Repeal or Suspension of the Law annulling the Charter of the Bank. Matthew Carey, Editor. Philadelphia, 1786.

Dissertations on Government, the Affairs of the Bank, and Paper Money, by Thomas Paine. Philadelphia, 1786.

The True Interest of the United States, and particularly of Pennsylvania, Considered, etc., with some

ruin and that of their creditors, by giving them the temporary use of credit and money. Its slender capital, as compared with the vastness of its transactions, rendered it merciless in the strict punctuality which it required of its debtors, thus frequently throwing honest men into the hands of usurers. The great dividends on bank stock induced moneyed men to invest in this way rather than lend to the public at a reasonable rate of interest. Rich foreigners would for the same reason be induced to buy up bank stock, until, finally, the whole capital of the institution would be owned abroad, and the country constantly drained of specie by the exportation of the dividends in coin. The bank injured the circulation of the State bills of credit. The directors were by their position enabled to obtain unfair advantages in trade for themselves and their friends. The wealth and influence of the corporation, and particularly its attribute of perpetual existence, were dangerous to the Government, and destructive of that equality which ought to exist in a free country.

Such were the chief arguments used by the Democratic party in favor of the repeal of the charter.

In answer to these, the supporters of the bank urged a variety of considerations. They admitted it to be true that some persons had been ruined by the help of a fictitious credit, but this they averred proceeded from the folly of the borrower, and not from the fault of the bank. His misfortune was a consequence not of the use, but of the abuse, of the privileges which the bank afforded. "It would be a marvellous thing to prohibit the use of water because some people choose to drown themselves."

1785

Observations on the Subject of a Bank, etc. Philadelphia, 1786. Political Essays, by Pelatiah Webster.

They conceded that the punctuality required by the bank was sometimes injurious in its result, yet they pointed out that the borrower should be more careful in calculating when he could repay, and that the bank should not be blamed for enforcing an agreement into which their customer had voluntarily entered. They denied that the bank stock in the market prevented investment in other directions. They showed how inconsiderable a proportion the capital of the bank bore to the floating cash of the country, and attributed the stringency of the money market rather to the drain of specie abroad, and to the fear of a paper issue, followed by a legal tender enactment, than to any causes over which the bank held control. They averred that the purchase of bank stock by foreigners was rather to be encouraged than dreaded. It was sure to bring specie into the country and to secure numerous friends abroad, who would dread nothing so much as the occurrence of a war with any European power. As to the exportation of dividends, they urged that this should constitute no cause for apprehension as long as the pru-

1785 cipal on which they were based remained among us. They admitted that the management of the bank had at first been opposed to the new emission of paper money, but insisted that the institution could now present no efficient obstacle to its circulation. They showed, indeed, that the directors had abandoned their former policy of opposition, and had lent what aid they could to the circulation of the new bills by freely receiving them on deposit. They challenged their opponents to adduce one single instance of undue favoritism on the part of the directors, and pointed out the absurdity of assigning the possibility of injustice as sufficient ground for divesting chartered rights. Finally, they contended that the institution, so far from being dangerous to the Government, had already proved itself of most material assistance to it. Nor could they understand how the existence of a corporation so beneficent in its operations could be deemed inconsistent with the principles of the Republic.

Other considerations were presented by the friends of the bank of equal, if not greater, weight. They claimed that Congress had not exceeded its powers in calling the corporation into existence; that a national bank had become a national necessity, and, as such, was properly created by the central national power. Implied authority to this end they claimed was conferred by the Articles of Confederation upon Congress by the clause enabling it to borrow money on the credit of the various States. Assuming, therefore, the validity of the Congressional Ordinance of Incorporation, they urged with great force that the repeal of the charter granted by the State would be nugatory, and that the bank would be enabled to continue business without interruption.

1785

Waiving this point, they insisted that the stockholders of the Bank of North America could not be constitutionally deprived of their property in their chartered rights without due compensation being made them by the State, or the institution of a judicial proceeding in the nature of a *quo warranto*. And even if it was competent for the Legislature thus to override private rights, they pointed out the folly of such an arbitrary exercise of power as sure to shake the confidence alike of our own people and foreign nations in the credit and honesty of the Commonwealth.

In addition, they recalled to the minds of the people the great and solid benefits which the bank had already conferred, its loans to the Government, its assistance to the State, its support to trade and commerce, its invaluable services in aiding to restore the country to a sound financial basis; and they expressed a hope that, if permitted to carry on its prosperous and increasing business, it would continue to perform for the

1785

Letter, Morris to Daniel Clarke, May 30, 1782. Diplomatic Correspondence, vol. xii. p. 168.

community the same beneficent offices of which experience had shown that it was capable. If thwarted in its prospects by legislative interference, a diminution in its sphere of usefulness was of course to be anticipated, but even then they ventured to predict that it would "exist in spite of calumny, operate in spite of opposition, and do good in spite of malevolence."

Journal of Assembly, March 21 and 23, 1785.

Meantime, a host of petitions for and against the proposed repeal were presented to the Assembly. About twelve hundred signatures urged the measure: about half as many opposed it.

Ibid., March 28, 1785.

The weight of popular opinion was too strong to be withstood. On March 28 the committee to whom the matter had been referred reported that in its opinion the bank as then managed was in every way inconsistent with the public safety, and it therefore recommended that a bill should be at once brought in to repeal the act of incorporation. It was in vain that the friends of the institution moved to substitute the phrase "alter or amend" for the word "repeal." The amendment was rejected by a two-thirds majority, the report accepted, and the committee at once reappointed to bring in a bill in accordance with its own recommendation. On the following day, March 29, the committee reported the bill to the House, and at the same time a most respectful memorial was read from the President and Directors of the Bank

Ibid., March 29, 1785.

of North America, praying that they might be heard by counsel against the proposed measure.

On April 4 the bill came up for second reading, and the House determined to push it with vigor. The bank was refused permission to be heard by counsel, a motion to postpone the consideration of the bill was lost, and by an overwhelming majority it was ordered to be transcribed and printed for public circulation and comment.

Journal of Assembly, April 4, 1785.

The House soon after adjourned, but the directors of the bank could now have little doubt what the fate of their charter would be. They resolved, therefore, to make application to Congress for some relief from their embarrassing position. James Wilson, one of their number, took upon himself the task. The following passage from a letter written to him on May 12, 1785, by the president, Mr. Willing, will best serve to indicate the tone of feeling then prevalent among the friends of the bank: "As to the business of the bank, the whole must be left to your prudence to take such steps in Congress as the magnitude of the question and the complexion of that body may render necessary and proper. 'Fiat justitia et contentus sum.' With the Assembly the word is 'Carthago est delenda,' let the Congress judge for what end or purpose, and let them consider too that when this political child of theirs has once breathed its last, they have no Promethean power to call another

1785 into existence: confidence once lost is not often, if ever, to be regained. This is, perhaps, the only instance where a politic body has been annihilated, and private interest and property violated, without the least charge of abuse of power or malpractice suggested, much less proved before a jury of twelve men. In the present case not only the Constitution of the State is violated, but the Confederation of all the States is also violated, and a stab—a mortal stab—is given to the honor of Congress and the credit of all America. We have served our country, and served her in the worst of times, when our present opposers gave no assistance to the means of doing it. Let them consider this, and blush at the return they are now making. Let the Congress, too, consider this, and then determine whether they ought not to exert their influence with every State to support an institution to which they have given an existence, and from which they have received a dutiful return. I have devoted a large portion of my time, and, considering the period of my life, a very precious part of it, too, to the service of my country in the establishment of the bank, but it is my pride, it is my greatest glory, that it has thus far succeeded. To preserve it from destruction, and to further our public measures, I would still go further, I would devote the few remaining years I have in its service rather than it should fall a sacrifice to the delusion of party, or to the insidious designs of Tories and British emissaries. God grant that this may not be the case. To prevent it, I conjure you, by every tie you have to the institution of which you were an early protector, by every tie you have to the country you live in, to exert every nerve in its defence."

<small>1785</small>

<small>From a copy in the possession of the bank.</small>

But no effectual steps were after all taken, and in August the Assembly of Pennsylvania again convened. A disposition was at once evinced to push through the bill repealing the bank's charter. On August 26, the first day of the session, an early day was named for the final disposition of the matter.

<small>Journal of Assembly, August 26, 1785.</small>

On the 30th a second memorial was presented from the President and Directors of the Bank, setting forth that, although their application to be heard at the last session of the House had failed, they were, nevertheless, not discouraged from renewing an application upon that subject, inasmuch as they apprehended that a hearing could not be denied them without violating both the essentials and forms of justice. The memorial further called to mind the great utility of the institution, both to the State and to individuals, and expressed a firm conviction that the petitioners would be able, if heard, to invalidate every objection that had been urged against it. They, therefore, prayed that they might be allowed, before any other proceedings were taken, to appear and present their case before the bar of the House.

1785
Journal of Assembly, August 30, 1785.

On the 31st the Assembly resolved to grant the prayer of the petition, but not without insisting that the hearing was of grace, not of right. At the same time they resolved that a like permission should be accorded to the advocates of the proposed repeal.

Ibid., August 31, 1785.

On September 5, accordingly, Mr. Willing appeared at the bar of the House, accompanied by James Wilson, Esq., whom he presented as authorized by the bank to speak in its defence. Mr. Wilson consumed the time of the House for the residue of that and a portion of the ensuing day, and was followed by Jonathan Dickinson Sergeant, Esq., who appeared on behalf of the petitioners. But the conclusion had long since been foregone. In the then state of popular prejudice Mr. Wilson's argument probably failed to convert the mind of a single member of the Assembly. On September 13 the bill was passed, and the bank as a State corporation ceased to exist.

Ibid., September 5 and 6, 1785.

Ibid., September 13, 1785.

Notwithstanding the deprivation of its corporate privileges, the bank continued to transact business, but naturally lost in some degree the confidence of moneyed men both at home and abroad. Its stock fell to six per cent. below par. Its cash account for 1784 had amounted in all to 59,570,000 Mexican dollars. For 1785 it dropped to 37,000,000 Mexi-

Letter, Thomas Willing to His Excellency P. J. Van Berckel and others, June 17, 1786, of which the bank retains a copy.

can dollars. But, in spite of all difficulties, by the close of the latter year its wealth was estimated at nine hundred thousand silver dollars.

In the month of March, 1786, a careful account was taken as to the ownership of its stock. It was found that this now aggregated in par value $870,400, or 2176 shares. Of these but 285 shares were owned by foreigners, nine-tenths of whom were Dutchmen, 606 shares were owned by citizens of New Hampshire, Massachusetts, Rhode Island, Connecticut, New York, New Jersey, Delaware, and Virginia, 50 shares were owned by Pennsylvanians resident in other parts of the State, and all those remaining, viz., 1235 shares, were owned by citizens of Philadelphia.

The continuance of the bank's operations was deemed on the part of the directors to be fully warranted by the powers derived from the Congressional charter. But, however confident they might be as to the validity of that instrument, they could not but be sensible that grave doubts on that point were entertained in the community.

Early, therefore, in January, 1786, they resolved to take steps to re-establish, if possible, their corporate existence under State sanction. Their counsel advised them that " the modification of the bank's charter, as to limitation of time or capital, would not at all affect the Congress charter, and that it would not be improper for them to

1785
Political Essays, by Pelatiah Webster, 447 and 449.

1786
Debates and Proceedings of the General Assembly of Pennsylvania on the Memorials praying a Repeal or Suspension of the Law annulling the Charter of the Bank. Matthew Carey, Editor. Philadelphia, 1786, 25.

68   A HISTORY OF

1786

Minutes of Stockholders' Meeting, January 9, 1786.

Booth's Laws of Delaware, vol. ii. 838.

Minutes of Directors, February 6, 1786.

receive such a charter." Overtures were, therefore, at once made to the State of Delaware for a grant of corporate rights, which were so successful that on February 2, 1786, the Assembly of that Commonwealth passed a bill conferring upon the bank the usual franchises of a corporation. On February 7 the directors received notice of this fact, and readily accepted the charter;[1] and, if necessary to the transaction of their business, they

---

[1] The following letter to Richard Bassett, Esq., of Delaware, whose efforts had been most active in the bank's behalf, was written by Mr. Willing immediately on receipt of the new charter:

BANK, Feb. the 6th, 1786.
RICHARD BASSETT, Esqr.

SIR,— I have this moment the Honor of yours of the 3d Inst., covering the Charter granted to the Bank of North America by the Patriotick Legislature of the Delaware State. It is too late this Evening to lay it before the Directors, and your Express is anxious to go off early in the morning. Therefore I can only say for myself that I feel in the highest Degree the Obligation the Institution is under to the State of Delaware for thus kindly taking us by the Hand and giving us their protection, at a Time when our misguided Assembly here have Attempted most unreasonably to crush and destroy us. I thank you for the Service you have done us on this Occasion, and you may depend on the Warmest Zeal on my part to render every Service to your State, and the many Worthy Individuals of it, whenever it falls within my Line of Duty, either in the station I have now the Honor to fill, or as an Inhabitant of Pennsylvania. I am, Sir, with the highest respect,

Yr much Obliged humb. St,
THOMAS WILLING, Prest.

A copy of the above letter is to be found among the archives of the bank.

actually contemplated the removal of the bank to Wilmington, New Castle, or some other proper point within the State of Delaware.

It was deemed wisest, however, before taking so desperate a step, and one which in all probability would interfere so materially with the prosperity and usefulness of the bank, to make every effort to induce the Assembly of Pennsylvania to reconsider its late action.

Accordingly, shortly after the reassembling of that body on March 3, 1786, a petition, signed by no less than 624 citizens of Philadelphia County, was presented and read, praying for an immediate repeal of the act rescinding the charter of the bank. The petitioners recited again at great length the former services of the institution to the Government and to the public, and insisted that the late proceedings of the Assembly were unjust and arbitrary in the extreme. They pointed out the haste with which the measure had been carried through the House, showed that the public had had no fair opportunity of canvassing its merits, urged that the bank should at least have been permitted to adduce evidence with respect to the charges that had been preferred against it, and finally, denied that those charges were actually true.

Petitions of like purport coming in daily, the matter was referred to a committee, whose report was taken up for discussion on March 29. It

1786

Journal of Assembly, March 3, 1786.

The committee reported March 23, 1786. See Journal of Assembly, eo die.

1786 revealed with great distinctness the motives by which the House had been actuated at the former session. It showed that neither the committee of investigation nor any of the prominent supporters of the bill had any practical acquaintance with the method of conducting the bank's operations. Although offered by the directors every facility, they had declined to make any inquiry into its affairs, or even to come within its walls, but had been guided wholly, as the committee thought, by general preconceived notions, and according to the current of popular opinion rather than by the dictates of sober reason. It was further the opinion of the committee that the former House had too much disregarded the ordinary legislative forms and delays, that it should have proceeded with far greater caution in so important a matter as the divesting of chartered rights, and that the result of its conduct was a measure which the committee conceived to have "its foundations deeply laid in injustice, and to remain a reproach both to the Government and the people." It then called attention to the eminent respectability and intelligence of the present petitioners, and concluded by recommending that a committee should be at once appointed to bring in an act repealing the obnoxious measure.

Journal of Assembly, March 29, 1786.

A very warm debate ensued, and lasted for three days. The petitioners for a reconsideration of the repealing act now amounted to nearly three thousand, and the supporters of the bank felt a corresponding encouragement. Messrs. Morris, Robinson, Clymer, and Fitzsimons were the chief advocates of the institution. Messrs. Whitehill, Findlay, Lollar, and Smiley its principal opponents. On the second day of the debate Robert Morris rose, and, in a speech of considerable length and consummate ability, defended the management from the charges of favoritism which had been made against them and demonstrated the value of their services to the Government and the community.

"I have," said he, "a perfect and thorough conviction that the institution in its operation, far from being injurious to the State, is of service to every individual in it. It promotes the grandeur of the State, increases its wealth, and adds to its dignity."

But the drift of popular prejudice was still too strong. On April 1 the House divided upon the question whether it should accept the report, and the decision was in the negative by a vote of 41 to 27. The minority unanimously entered their dissent upon the minutes, and a few days after brought forward a resolution looking to the suspension of the repealing act. But this also met with no favor, and for the remainder of the session the matter was allowed to drop.

1786

Debates and Proceedings of the General Assembly of Pennsylvania on the Memorials praying the Repeal or Suspension of the Law annulling the Charter of the Bank. Matthew Carey, Editor. Philadelphia, 1786, &c.

Journal of Assembly, April 1, 1786.

Ibid., April 7, 1786.

1786

Journal of Assembly, November 16, 1786.

Ibid., November 29, 1786.

In November the Assembly again came together, and the subscribers to the bank again presented a memorial praying the House to reconsider its hasty and ill-advised action, setting forth anew with tedious minuteness the same arguments which had been before so often urged. Their efforts were at length to be crowned with success. The memorial was referred to a committee, who, on November 29, presented their report, as follows:

"That it is consistent with the policy of the Government immediately to revive the charter of the bank, but as this charter, altogether unlimited in duration, and almost so in the capital stock allowed to be employed, may from these circumstances become an object of jealousy and apprehension, your committee are of opinion that it might be expedient to qualify it, in its revival, in these respects, but in such manner as that, while all reasonable ground of objection to an institution so eminently useful to the commerce and agriculture of the State is removed, the bank shall remain uninjured in its essential rights, and be left freely to its own operations."

Ibid., December 13, 1786.

Ibid., December 15, 1786.

On December 13 a committee was appointed to draw up a bill such as was recommended. On the 15th the bill was introduced, and, in spite of some opposition and numerous memorials against its passage, reached by the middle of March, 1787, its final stages. On the 17th of that month it was finally agreed to by a vote of thirty-five to twenty-eight.

1787
Journal of Assembly, March 17, 1787.

The terms of the new charter differed materially from those which had preceded it. The corporate existence of the bank was limited to a term of fourteen years, and its wealth restricted to two million of dollars. It was forbidden to hold real estate, except in so far as was necessary for the transaction of its business and the prevention of loss on its investments. It was expressly prohibited from trading in any merchandise, save bullion and bills of exchange. Finally, it was to cause copies of all its by-laws, as passed from time to time, to be deposited with the State authorities.

Act of March 17, 1787. 2 Dallas' Laws, 499.

Although far from satisfied with the provisions of the bill, the directors of the bank conceived it best to act under its provisions, a step which, as will be seen hereafter, certainly sacrificed whatever rights they may have previously obtained from Congress.

The bank may now be fairly said to have passed through the most critical period of its existence. Peace had for some time been re-established, and the disastrous effects of the war were at least in some measure beginning to disappear. A dangerous and turbulent opposition had been successfully overcome, and the utility of the institution thor-

1788

1788 oughly demonstrated. Its notes continued to circulate at their full value, the difficulties that had environed it vanished, and all fears respecting its ability to redeem its promises subsided.

Encouraged by its success, two other banks—one in New York,[1] the other in Boston[2]—had already sprung into existence. In 1791[3] a fourth was established at Providence, and in 1795[4] a fifth at Baltimore. The banking system had obtained a foothold in the country.

[1] The Bank of New York began business in 1784, but was not chartered till March 21, 1791.

[2] The Bank of Massachusetts was chartered February 7, 1784.

[3] The Providence Bank went into operation in October, 1791. 5 Collections of Historical Society of Rhode Island, 357.

[4] Scharf's Chronicles of Baltimore, 260.

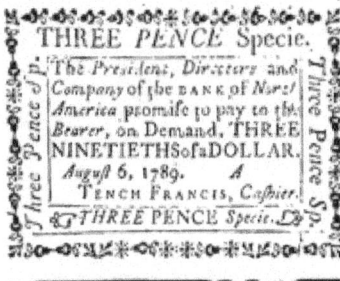

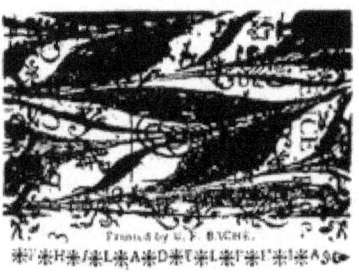

CHAPTER V.

1789-1809.

The Constitution of the United States goes into effect in March, 1789—Hamilton's Treasury Report of 1790—Reasons for the Establishment of the Bank of the United States—The Bank of North America unable and unwilling to discharge the Functions of such an Institution—Resignation of Thomas Willing as President in 1792—Election of John Nixon as President—Business of the Bank in 1792—Establishment of the Bank of Pennsylvania in 1793—The Whiskey Insurrection of 1794—Business of the Bank in 1794 and 1795—The Yellow Fever of 1798—Temporary Removal of the Bank to Germantown—Renewal of the Charter in 1799—Increase in the Number of Banking Institutions—Reform in the Bank's Method of transacting Business effected in 1806—Establishment of the Surplus Fund in 1809—Death of John Nixon and Election of John Morton as President in 1809.

IN March, 1789, a great and fortunate change took place in the management of public affairs. The Constitution of the United States went into operation. A vigorous, responsible executive was conferred upon the country, and an incredible impulse given to all schemes of national importance. Among those now called upon to take part in the administration of public affairs was Alexander Hamilton. Placed in charge of the Department

1789

1789 of the Treasury, he found before him the prodigious task of settling the financial affairs of the United States upon a sure and satisfactory basis. Towards the attainment of this end no measure seemed more important to him than his old and favorite one for the establishment of a great national bank. Without loss of time he devised a plan for such an institution, which seemed to him practicable, and in 1790 spread before Congress the result of his labors.

1790

Treasury Report of 1790. Hamilton's Works, vol. iii. 126.

The proposed measure met generally with popular applause, but there were some who doubted its wisdom. Among other difficulties that were thrown in its path was a suggestion that a new bank was quite unnecessary, since an institution was in existence which owed its origin to national bounty, and which had already, upon more than one occasion, manifested both its readiness and ability to extend a helping hand to the Government. With this objection Hamilton dealt most courteously.

"The aid afforded to the United States," said he, "by the Bank of North America during the remaining period of the war was of essential consequence, and its conduct towards them since the peace has not weakened its title to their patronage and favor. So far its pretensions to the character of a national bank are respectable, but there are circumstances which militate against them, and considerations which indicate the propriety of an establishment on different principles.

"The directors of this bank, on behalf of their constituents, have since acted under a new charter from the State of Pennsylvania, materially variant from their original one; and which so narrows the foundation of the institution as to render it an incompetent basis for the extensive purposes of a national bank. . . .

"There is nothing in the acts of Congress which imply an exclusive right in the institution to which they relate, except during the time of the War. There is, therefore, nothing, if the public good require it, which prevents the establishment of another. It may, however, be incidentally remarked, that in the general opinion of the citizens of the United States, the Bank of North America has taken the station of a bank of Pennsylvania only. This is a strong argument for a new institution, or for a renovation of the old, to restore it to the situation in which it originally stood in the view of the United States. But . . . there may be room to allege that the Government of the United States ought not, in point of candor or equity, to establish any rival or interfering institution in prejudice of the one already established, especially as this has, from services rendered, well-founded claims to protection and regard.

"The justice of this observation ought, within

'1790 proper bounds, to be admitted. A new establishment of the sort ought not to be made without cogent and sincere reasons of public good. And, in the manner of doing it, every facility should be given to a consolidation of the old with the new, upon terms not injurious to the parties concerned. But there is no ground to maintain that in a case in which the Government has made no condition restricting its authority, it ought voluntarily to restrict it, through regard to the interests of a particular institution, when those of the State dictate a different course; especially too after such circumstances have intervened, as characterize the actual situation of the Bank of North America. . . .

"If the objections, which have been stated, to the constitution of the Bank of North America, are admitted to be well founded, they will, nevertheless, not derogate from the merit of the main design, or of the services which that bank has rendered, or of the benefits which it has produced. The creation of such an institution, at the time it took place, was a measure dictated by wisdom. Its utility has been amply evinced by its fruits. American independence owes much to it. . . .

"The Secretary begs leave to conclude with this general observation, that if the Bank of North America shall come forward with any propositions, which have for their object the ingrafting upon that institution the characteristics which shall appear to the Legislature necessary to the due extent and safety of a national bank, there are, in his judgment, weighty inducements to giving every reasonable facility to the measure. Not only the pretensions of that institution, from its original relation to the Government of the United States, and from the services it has rendered, are such as to claim a disposition favorable to it, if those who are interested in it are willing, on their part, to place it on a footing satisfactory to the Government, and equal to the purposes of a bank of the United States; but its co-operation would naturally accelerate the accomplishment of the great object, and the collision, which might otherwise arise, might, in a variety of ways, prove equally disagreeable and injurious. The incorporation and union here contemplated may be effected in different modes, under the auspices of an act of the United States, if it shall be desired by the Bank of North America, upon terms which shall appear expedient to the Government."

1790

Treasury Report of 1790. Hamilton's Works, vol. iii. 126.

As far as can be ascertained, however, the management of the bank took no steps in accordance with the suggestions of the report. The quiet and prosperous business in which they were engaged, under State auspices, was to them preferable to the anxieties and hazards which would probably attend the new national undertaking. The scheme of a separate institution was, therefore, rapidly

1791

1791	pushed forward, and on February 19, 1791, the first Bank of the United States began its corporate existence.
1792	The Bank of North America now sustained a serious loss in the resignation of its president, Mr. Willing, on January 9, 1792, after a term of service extending over a little more than ten years. He had been chosen to preside over the affairs of the Bank of the United States, a station for which it was justly supposed that his talents and experience eminently qualified him. He was succeeded in office by John Nixon, an almost equally well-known and respected citizen. Born in 1733 of Irish parentage, Mr. Nixon for a number of years did a prosperous business in the city of Philadelphia. He was one of the many signers of the Non-Importation Resolutions, and upon the breaking out of the Revolution made himself prominent by his strenuous efforts and warm interest in the national cause. He was a member of the Committee of Safety, and had the honor of first proclaiming to the citizens of Philadelphia the Declaration of Independence. During some portion of the war he did active service, with the rank of colonel, in the Continental army. He was one of the original subscribers to the bank, and had been a director since 1784. He retained the office of president for seventeen years until his death, which occurred on December 24, 1808.

An interesting sketch of the career of John Nixon will be found in the "Centennial Collection." 1 Pennsylvania Magazine of History and Biography, 188.

PRESIDENT OF THE BANK OF NORTH AMERICA
1792 1808

Meantime, the business of the bank was rapidly increasing as the commerce of the country grew. The profits were so great that annual dividends of twelve per cent. were paid to the various stockholders. Nor did the institution cease to accommodate the public from time to time with loans of considerable extent. During the year 1791 the bank advanced to the Commonwealth, at different times, in all $160,000, and in the following year something over $53,000.

In 1793 the State made some overtures to the bank, with a view of becoming a participant in its business and profits, but a satisfactory arrangement, it was found, could not be concluded. The result of these negotiations was the establishment of the first rival institution with which the Bank of North America had to contend on its own ground. The State authorities, having been unsuccessful in their application to the old bank for an interest in its dealings, now obtained from the Legislature a charter for an entirely new institution, known as the Bank of Pennsylvania, in which the Commonwealth was interested to the extent of a million of dollars. By a clause in the act of incorporation the stockholders of the Bank of North America, upon relinquishing their charter, were at liberty to embark their whole capital in the new undertaking. But of this permission they declined to avail themselves.

1792

Directors' Minutes, August 16, 1792, also Stockholders' Minutes, January and February, 1793.

1793

Act March 30, 1793, 3 Smith's Laws, 97.

Stockholders' Minutes, May 28, 1793.

1794

Directors'
Minutes,
September
15, 1794, and
December 8,
1794.

Ibid., January 12, 1795.

1795

Ibid., December 21, 1796.

1798

In 1794, the Whiskey Insurrection, which for three years had been going on in the western part of the State, reached its climax. In the fall an army of 19,500 men was sent against the insurgents, to whose equipment there is reason to think the bank materially contributed. The notes of all persons actually on military service were by the bank on application laid over or renewed, nor was any demand made for their payment until the conclusion of peace.

During the year 1794 the business of the bank increased to an unprecedented extent. The whole amount of the year's debits and credits exceeded 240 millions, and the amount of cash received and paid, as entered in the cash-book, 120 millions, exclusive of several millions passing in exchange with other banks, and also of large sums of gold and silver exchanged for notes, and of notes exchanged for specie, not appearing on the books. During the following year the transactions were even larger, the books showing that the amount of cash received and paid was more than 121 millions.

In the summer of 1798 the prevalence of the yellow fever caused the bank to alter the site of its operations. So disastrous were the ravages of the disease in the neighborhood of the banking-house, that by September it was thought unsafe for the clerks to attend to their daily duties. On September 5 a meeting of the directors was accord-

ingly convened at the cashier's house in the Northern Liberties, in such haste that the minute-book was forgotten, being left behind in the bank, and it was resolved immediately to transfer the business to Germantown.

For this purpose the Union School-House was leased in common by the Banks of North America and Pennsylvania, and on the 6th instant the former moved into its new quarters. Here the transactions of the bank were carried on for nearly two months. Meantime, the distress in the city was incredible. Multitudes died, business was to a large degree suspended, and the poor were reduced to the greatest straits by the lack of employment. The bank advanced $10,000 in aid of the sufferers, which proved of material assistance. By November 2 the malady had so far subsided that the bank was enabled to resume its business in town.

In 1801 the charter of the bank expired. By this time, however, the Legislature had come to appreciate somewhat more fully the value of the institution, and there was, therefore, but little trouble in procuring a renewal of its corporate franchises for a further term of fourteen years. This was effected by an act of Assembly approved March 20, 1799.

The bank now continued its business for several years under auspices less favorable than before.

1798

Directors' Minutes, September 5 and 6, 1798.

Ibid., September 10, 1798.

Ibid., November 2, 1798.

1801

3 Smith's Laws, 359.

1804

Observations on the Principles and Operations of Banking, with Strictures on the Opposition to the Bank of Philadelphia, 1804, 16.

1806

The number of banks in the country had greatly increased. By 1804 it was estimated that there were forty-five in active operation. Trade and commerce had received an immense impetus, and the methods of doing business were rapidly and materially altered. The Bank of North America was under a management too conservative to keep pace with these innovations, and, as a consequence, by 1806 its profits were sensibly decreased.

A committee appointed to make investigation into the causes of this decline reported that it was to be attributed to a variety of circumstances. In the first place, the policy of the bank had for the past few years been such as to prevent it from partaking in any great degree of that patronage from the General and State Governments which other banks enjoyed. In addition to this, it appeared that for many years the directors had been in the habit of discounting large amounts of accommodation-paper, which they renewed from time to time, as a matter of course, thus making a great part of the bank's capital comparatively inoperative. Nor was the benefit of these loans shared at all equally by the mercantile community. On the contrary, the accommodation was afforded almost exclusively to a few favored individuals, who were familiar with the character of the bank's operations.

A vigorous attempt was made to do away with these evils by the speedy adoption of measures of

PRESIDENT OF THE BANK OF NORTH AMERICA
1803-1822

reform. Credits were shortened, the punctual collection of debts more rigorously enforced, discounts upon accommodation-paper at long dates rejected in favor of investments which promised more profit and less delay, and the advantages to be derived from the use of the capital thus more generally thrown open to the mercantile world.

So successful were these efforts that within a few years the bank regained all its former prosperity. By the close of 1809 it was enabled to begin a surplus fund by the laying aside of $15,000 of the profit and loss account. To this was added $27,400, a sum realized from the sale of some of the bank shares which had not before been subscribed for. Others of these shares were now sold, enough to make the sum in all of $80,000, and it was agreed that the annual interest on this amount should be accumulated until the fund reached $100,000.

The year 1809 was also marked in the history of the bank by the election of a new president. John Nixon died on December 24, 1808, and, at the first meeting held by the incoming board of directors for the year 1809, John Morton was unanimously elected in his place.

1806

Directors' Minutes, November 17, 1806.

1809

Ibid., December 18, 1809.

Ibid., January 10, 1809.

CHAPTER VI.

1810-1846.

Expiration of the Charter of the First Bank of the United States—The Bank of North America Petitions Congress for the Renewal in 1810—Failure to obtain a Renewal from Congress—The War of 1812—Assistance afforded by the Bank to the Government during the War—The Panic of 1814—Policy of the Bank during the Panic—Renewal of the Bank's Charter in 1814—Establishment of the Second Bank of the United States—End of the Panic in 1817—Resignation of John Morton from the Presidency in 1822 and Election of Henry Nixon in his place—Renewal of the Charter in 1825—Terms of the New Charter—Sale of the Bank Shares in 1825—Efforts to obtain a Renewal of the Charter of the Second Bank of the United States in 1832—Attitude of the Bank of North America—Failure of the Efforts—Change in the Method of Transacting the Bank's Business between 1830 and 1835—The Congressional Charter Null and Void—Failure of Efforts to obtain an Increase of the Capital Stock in 1835—The Panic of 1837—Suspension of Specie Payments—Policy of the Bank of North America—Death of Henry Nixon in 1840, and Election of John Richardson as President—Resumption of Specie Payments in January, 1841—Failure of the Bank of the United States in February, 1841—Renewed Suspension of Specie Payments—The "Relief Act" of May 4, 1841—Refusal of the Bank of North America to accept its Terms—Views of the Bank as to Resumption—Resumption effected in March, 1842—Dangerous Position of the Bank in 1842—

Reduction of its Capital in 1843—Restoration of the Capital to its old Volume in 1845—Renewal of the Charter in 1846—Provisions of the New Charter.

In 1810, the charter of the first Bank of the United States being about to expire, a bill was introduced into Congress providing for its renewal. The measure had many advocates, but more determined opponents. In December, the fate of the bill being very doubtful, a host of memorials and petitions flowed in from all sides both for and against its passage. The directors of the Bank of North America strongly urged the necessity of the renewal. They transmitted to Congress a memorial, averring that in their opinion the termination of the national bank's operations would be attended with great suffering on the part of the commercial and agricultural interest, both on account of the rapid collection of debts necessary to wind up its affairs, and the loss of so valuable an institution. The citizens of Pennsylvania, in particular, they represented, would suffer great distress. They were borrowers from the bank to a large amount, and owned fully a million of its capital stock; their sacrifices must therefore be enormous if the charter were allowed to expire. Finally, the petitioners pointed out the past services of the institution, and expressed serious apprehensions as to how the commerce of the country was to be carried on without its co-operation and assistance.

1810

Directors' Minutes, December 31, 1810.

1811 But, notwithstanding all argument, the bill was thrown out by the House. A similar one failed in the Senate, and on March 4, 1811, the first Bank of the United States ceased to exist.

1812 In 1812 war was declared with Great Britain. The Government at once had recourse to loans to support the army and navy, depending principally upon the banks to supply these, as well as to assist in promoting the circulation of the Treasury notes. The Bank of North America was prompt to afford assistance in both directions. It received and circulated the Government notes, opened subscription-books in its banking-room to the United States loan of 1813, and advanced to the Government in all about $650,000 before the close of 1815, besides affording material aid to the defence of the city.

Goddard's History of Banking Institutions in Europe and America, 129 et seq.

Directors' Minutes, July 26, 1815.

1813

Ibid., March 21, 1813.

Ibid., April 27, 1812, May 15 and June 19, 1815.

In common with the other banks, it suffered severely from the disastrous system of over-issues and excessive trading into which the country then 1814 plunged, and in August, 1814, it was finally forced with them to suspend the payment of specie.

In the conferences which were now held between the various Philadelphia banks, the Bank of North America took a leading part. It advocated from the first a more decisive and consistent line of policy than any other bank, advising the immediate contraction of issues and cutting down of discounts, so as to insure resumption at an early and definite day. But it was not until February 20, 1817, and then largely through the assistance of the second Bank of the United States, which had in the mean time been chartered, that the banks found themselves strong enough to accomplish this result.

In the year 1813, the period stipulated by the bank's charter having nearly expired, application had been made to the Legislature for a further extension. But this was not to be had on very favorable terms. On March 28, 1814, an act was finally approved which renewed the bank's chartered existence for a term of ten years. In addition to the limitations of the former charter several new ones were now inserted. The capital was restricted to one million of dollars, and no stock was to be transferred to or held by aliens, except citizens of Holland. Its affairs were at all times to be open to Legislative scrutiny. In addition to this, the bank, as a consideration for its franchise, was to pass $120,000 to the credit of the State upon its books, and the Legislature was to be at liberty at any time to annul the charter on refunding a proportional part of this bonus. At a meeting of the stockholders held May 11, 1814, the charter was formally accepted, and the stipulated sum was shortly after paid to the State.

A period now ensued of tolerable commercial

[margin notes:]
1814
Directors' Minutes, September 4 and October 19, 1815.

Ibid., February 3, 1817.

Ibid., November 2, 1812.

Act, March 28, 1814. Pamphlet Laws, 281.
Stockholders' Minutes, May 11, 1814.

<small>1822</small>

<small>Directors'
Minutes,
January 15,
1822.</small>

<small>1825</small>

<small>Directors'
Minutes,
January 24,
1825.</small>

prosperity, during which the bank did a fair average business. In 1822, John Morton resigned the office of president, and was succeeded by Henry Nixon, son of John Nixon, the second president of the institution.

In 1825, the charter being again about to expire, application was again made to the Legislature for its renewal. The directors desired, if possible, to secure to the corporation the right to hold real estate, which was withheld by the former charter, and to have the clause authorizing investigation into the bank's affairs by the Legislature omitted, but in neither of these respects were they successful.

The new charter, indeed, which was approved March 21, 1825, imposed a variety of new limitations and qualifications upon the corporate powers. The title of the corporation was now for the first time changed to "The Bank of North America."[1] The debts incurred were never to exceed twice the amount of the capital, and, in case they did, the directors consenting to such excess were to be personally liable. The discounts were never to exceed the rate of one-half per cent. a month. Dividends were invariably to be declared at least once in the year. In case of the non-payment of specie, a

---

[1] Its title had theretofore been "The President, Directors, and Company of the Bank of North America." See *ante*, page 35.

PRESIDENT OF THE BANK OF NORTH AMERICA
1822-1840

speedy method was provided for the forfeiture of the charter. In such event, at any rate, no new notes were to be issued, except to depositors of a corresponding amount of specie. Not only was the Legislature to be at full liberty to investigate into the bank's affairs, but at stipulated intervals a carefully prepared statement of its accounts was to be submitted to the State authorities. Upon these terms the bank was incorporated anew until April 1, 1847, with the usual corporate franchises. It was to pay as compensation eight per cent. per annum of its dividend to the Commonwealth, and was also to loan, on sixty days' notice, at any time, a twentieth part of its paid in capital to the State, at the rate of five per cent. The bank accepted the new charter, and continued business under its provisions.

In September, 1825, the directors resolved to dispose of the shares in the bank which the institution itself still held, so as to increase the capital to the chartered limit of one million of dollars. In this way 414 shares were sold, which were worth at par $165,600, and which, being disposed of at their market value, brought the bank in a profit of over $33,000.

About the year 1830 began the contest relative to the renewal of the charter of the second Bank of the United States. In 1832 the stockholders of that institution declared their intention to apply to

1825

Act, March 21, 1825. 8 Smith's Laws, 386.

Directors' Minutes, June 16, 1825.

Ibid., September 19, 1825.

Ibid., June 27, 1825; June 30, 1825; October 6, 1825.

1830

1832

1832 Congress for an extension of their corporate existence. In this step they were warmly seconded by the management of the Bank of North America. "We are ready," said they, "to acknowledge, and we do so with great pleasure, that the Bank of the United States has hitherto accomplished the objects for which it was instituted,—in the resumption of specie payments under the most embarrassing circumstances, in the restoration of a sound currency to the country, in the equalization, as far as practicable, of our domestic exchanges, and in affording that kind and salutary protection to the State institutions of a similar character, which has acted like a balance to the great commercial machine, affording assistance to the associations acting upon sound banking principles, and checking the erratic course of those who, in too great a desire to extend their profits, might be induced to exceed the bounds of prudence. . . . We cannot with propriety forbear to express our fears that, unless the Bank of the United States should be rechartered, we may witness scenes of unparalleled commercial distress and embarrassment, which will be felt not only in the palaces of the rich but in the cottages of the poor, the enterprising, and the industrious." They tendered, therefore, their best wishes for the success of the bank in its application, and declared their willingness to co-operate with it in any proper way which would seem likely to effect a result so

Directors' Minutes, January 5, 1832.

important to the welfare and prosperity of the nation. 1832

The measure, though it met with vast opposition, passed both Houses of Congress, and was only defeated by the interposition of the Presidential veto. The administration, flushed with this success, now prepared a second and almost equally crushing blow to the bank's prospects. In September, 1833, it suddenly withdrew the public deposits from the bank's vaults, and placed them in the custody of other banks the management of which was more in consonance with President Jackson's views. A storm of opposition was at once awakened. Among others, the Bank of North America transmitted an indignant memorial to the members of Congress, praying that they would order a return of the deposits to the Bank of the United States "as a sure mode of restoring confidence and credit to the community." Resolutions of this purport were actually passed both in the Senate and the House, but with no effect on the persistent opposition of the administration. 1833

<small>Directors' Minutes, December 19 1833.</small>

During the period intervening between 1830 and 1835 a great change took place in the method of conducting the bank's affairs. Business was very active, a thousand new industries were developing themselves in all parts of the country, and the need of banking capital was pressing in the extreme. But the operations of the bank had for 1835

1835

many years past been carried on upon a limited scale and by antiquated methods, so that the directors now found themselves unable to compete successfully with many of the new banking institutions which were growing up around them. Fortunately, just at this crisis a material change took place in the board of directors. A number of gentlemen, who were well advanced in years, either resigned or died, and their places were supplied by others who were more perfectly acquainted with the requirements of modern business. Under their auspices important reforms were speedily inaugurated, and the bank soon restored to a prominent position in the mercantile transactions of the time.

So extensive was the business now done by the bank that the directors in 1833 seriously began to consider the advisability of widening the sphere of its usefulness by an increase of the capital stock. The first thought was that perhaps this might be effected in pursuance of the original Congressional charter. But the design was soon abandoned. The charter in question was submitted to eminent counsel for their opinion as to the continued existence of the powers conferred thereby. That opinion was most distinctly adverse. "We think," said the gentlemen consulted, "that neither the bank nor the stockholders have any corporate faculties or capacities but such as are derived from

Directors' Minutes, February 11, 1833.

The counsel to whom the Congressional charter was submitted were James S. Smith, Esq., Horace Binney, Esq., and John Sergeant, Esq.

the laws of Pennsylvania, and that no act they can do can confer or revive any other corporate faculties or capacities."

Another course was therefore adopted. In December, 1835, it was resolved to petition the Legislature to authorize an increase of the capital stock to three millions of dollars. It was pointed out that the charter of the Bank of the United States would expire in the following March, and that the demand for banking capital would then have to be supplied from other sources. Hence it was argued that the Legislature could entertain no reasonable doubt as to the utility and propriety of the proposed extension. So earnest was the wish of the bank to succeed in this measure that the president was despatched to Harrisburg, and there remained for some time in order to "nurse the bill." It failed, however, fortunately for the bank, to secure the favor of the Legislature.

In the spring of the year 1837 the unparalleled business prosperity of the past few years ended in a panic of alarming magnitude. On May 10 the banks in New York generally suspended specie payments. On the 11th the banks in Philadelphia were forced to follow their example. The Bank of North America at once resolved to put itself in a fit posture for resumption. Resolutions were immediately introduced into the board of directors calculated to bring about a constant

1835
Directors' Minutes, November 11, 1835.

Ibid., December 15 and 31, 1835.

1836
Ibid., Feb. 1 and 8, 1836.

1837

Ibid., May 11, 1837.

<small>1837</small>
<small>Directors' Minutes, May 15, 1837.</small>

reduction in the amount of the outstanding loans, a policy which was steadily persevered in, as far as the circumstances and capabilities of the borrowers would warrant.

<small>1838</small>

By May of the year 1838 the city banks felt strong enough to attempt a partial resumption. At the recommendation of the convention of bank delegates they unanimously resolved that on and after May 9 they would pay all fractional parts of dollars in checks in coin, and, further, that they would redeem in coin on presentation all notes issued by the City and County of Philadelphia, or by any of the incorporated districts within the county limits.

<small>Ibid., May 9, 1838.</small>

By July 5, so far had public confidence been restored, that the 13th of the following August was finally fixed upon as the date when all the banks would return to a specie basis. Nor was there much difficulty, even among the weaker institutions, in accomplishing this result.

<small>1839</small>

The resumption was, however, only temporary. At a convention of the delegates of the banks in Philadelphia, held October 8, 1839, a proposition was made by the delegates of the Schuylkill Bank that the city banks generally should again decline to meet their obligations in specie. The measure was defeated, by a vote of nine banks to five, the Bank of North America casting its ballot in the negative. But the next day notice was received

PRESIDENT OF THE BANK OF NORTH AMERICA
1840-1857

that the Bank of the United States had agreed to suspend, and that the Philadelphia Bank and the Farmers and Mechanics' Bank had followed its example. The Bank of North America was, of course, forced to take similar action, though, unlike many of the other banking institutions, it continued to redeem in coin its own notes of a denomination of $5 or under.

1839

Directors'
Minutes,
October 9,
1839.

On August 18, 1840, Henry Nixon, the president of the bank, died. He had served the institution for nearly eighteen years. On September 3, 1840, John Richardson was elected to the office, the duties of which he continued to discharge for nearly seventeen years.

1840

Ibid., September 3, 1840.

Meantime, although the banks were generally preparing to resume, much distress and actual suffering were entailed on the community by reason of their suspension.

The banking laws of the State imposed severe penalties, and prescribed various disabilities, upon all banks who should fail to meet their obligations in specie. By the terms of the charter of the Bank of North America that institution was during the period of its suspension subject at any time to be deprived of its franchises by proclamation of the Executive of the Commonwealth, and, in addition to this, was strictly forbidden to make any new loans, to declare any dividends, or to issue any of its own notes, except to depositors who might demand them.

Pamphlet
Laws, 1825,
85.

1840 in lieu of their deposits. Somewhat similar provisions had been inserted in the charters of most of the other Pennsylvania banks. It may, therefore, be readily conceived how great and how well founded was the prevailing apprehension. Not only were all the banks liable at one blow to be swept out of existence, but they were unable to distribute dividends to their stockholders, advance loans to their customers, or afford a medium of exchange for the community, without directly contravening the provisions of the charters to which they owed their existence.

Pamphlet Laws, 714.

The Legislature was, therefore, forced to intervene. By an act approved April 3, 1840, the banks were given until January 15, 1841, to resume the payment of specie, and until that time they were exempted from the penalties imposed upon suspending banks, and enabled to issue their own notes, to grant loans, and to declare dividends, provided, however, that the latter did not exceed six per cent. per annum upon the capital stock.

Towards the close of the year the banks again began to make preparations to resume. The Bank of the United States alone seemed unequal to the task. The other banks of the city therefore advanced to it a temporary loan of five millions of dollars, which it was hoped would rescue it from its

Directors' Minutes, October 21, 1840.

embarrassments. The proportion of this amount furnished by the Bank of North America was

$400,000, and for this sum it was given post-notes, payable at the expiration of eighteen months.

1840

On January 15, 1841, the city banks generally complied with the requirements of the act of Assembly, and announced their intention to redeem all their liabilities in specie. But the favorable expectations of the community were doomed again to be disappointed. At the expiration of just three weeks from the general resumption, the Bank of the United States a third time suspended, declared itself unable to meet the demands of its creditors, and so ended its long and chequered career. Its assets were found to consist of a great mass of securities, some worthless, and some, in the disturbed financial condition of the country, absolutely inconvertible. Certain of these assets were placed in the hands of trustees to discharge the loan of five millions of dollars already mentioned, but it was many years before their cash value was realized and the loan entirely repaid.

1841

Directors' Minutes, February 4, 1841.

Report of Comptroller of Currency of United States, 1876, 15.

A meeting of the delegates from the Philadelphia banks was summoned on February 4, to take into consideration the best course for the banks to pursue. They recommended the continuance of specie payments, but the scheme was found impracticable. On the following day every bank in Philadelphia announced its intention to suspend, at least to some extent. The Bank of North America declared itself willing to redeem its five,

1841

Directors' Minutes, February 5, 1841.

ten, twenty, and fifty-dollar notes in coin, but as to the rest of its liabilities declined to meet them in the same manner.

All the distresses and anxieties occasioned by the stringency of the laws against suspension were now felt anew. The banks were again rendered liable to the prescribed penalties, and were in constant fear of forfeiture of their charters. But few new bank-notes were put in circulation. Scarcely any assistance was afforded by the banks to the mercantile community. Nor could the stockholders see any reasonable prospect of realizing dividends from their investments in the capital stock. To crown all, the credit of the State had begun to fail. The taxes levied in 1840 had very far fallen short of the amount necessary to pay the interest on the State loans. In addition to this there was a large sum owing for public improvements, which had been commenced in the prosperous times before 1837, and which were now left, many of them half completed, a burden in the hands of the Commonwealth.

17 Scribner's Monthly Magazine, 691.

In order to meet these vast expenses the Legislature enacted a bill, which has generally been termed the "Relief Act," the purpose of which was to extort from the banks of the Commonwealth a large advance to the State Treasury. By the provisions of this act a State loan of three million one hundred thousand dollars was authorized, payable at the expiration of five years, and bearing interest at the rate of five per cent. per annum. Any bank in the Commonwealth was to be at liberty to subscribe to this loan to the extent of seventeen and a half per cent. of its paid in capital. Payment was to be made to the State in notes of the bank to the amount subscribed. As long as these notes remained outstanding the bank was to receive from the State interest at the rate of one per cent. upon the loan. But on presentation of these notes at the bank a corresponding amount of the State loan was to be issued to the holder, upon which the bank was to remain liable for five per cent. interest until paid. The notes thus issued were to be receivable for debts due the Commonwealth, and could be reissued either from the State Treasury or from the bank issuing them.

In addition to this, any bank in the Commonwealth was enabled, on the deposit of State loan with the Treasurer of the Commonwealth, to an amount of not less than five and not more than seven per cent. of its paid in capital, to issue a like amount of its own notes, but interest was to be entirely suspended on the stock so deposited. Any bank complying with both the foregoing provisions was relieved and exempted from all penalties and forfeitures theretofore imposed for suspension of the payment of specie. If, on the contrary, any bank should decline within forty days to accept

1841

Pamphlet Laws, 307.

both of these provisions, it was declared to remain subject to all the penalties and forfeitures in case of suspension provided by existing laws. Governor Porter vetoed this bill, but on its return to the Legislature more than two-thirds of each House pronounced in its favor, and on May 4, 1841, it was enacted into a law.

Most of the Pennsylvania banks were only too glad to purchase immunity on the stipulated terms. But in this course they were not followed by the Bank of North America. A careful consideration of the provisions of the act satisfied the management that the bank would have everything to lose and nothing to gain by their acceptance. One hundred and seventy-five thousand dollars would in that event have to be invested in the five per cent. loan, and at least fifty thousand dollars of State loan deposited with the Government. In return, the bank would be at liberty to issue $225,000 of notes, $175,000 of which would have to be paid into the Treasury of the State, while the remaining $50,000 could be paid over the counter. But little, if any, profit could be expected from either of these issues. As to the $50,000, the bank would have to pay five per cent. interest to the State for the privilege of issuing it, by reason of the cessation in the payment of interest on the corresponding amount of State loan deposited with the Treasurer; and even if the bank should succeed in loaning the whole amount to customers at the rate of six per cent., thus yielding a profit of one per cent., the trifling sum of $3000 per annum alone would be realized, from which was to be deducted the expense of preparing the notes and sustaining them in circulation.

As to the $175,000, there seemed little chance of anything but absolute loss. Upon the redemption of the notes issued for that sum, the burden upon the bank must inevitably assume one of two forms,—either the holding of the five per cent. loan until repaid, thus abstracting almost one-fifth of the capital, or else an assumption of an obligation for the payment of the interest thereon, thus creating a mortgage of indefinite duration on the assets of the bank.

"The banks of this city cannot be justified," said the directors, "in parting with more of their available means. Causes well known to all have forced the most prudent of the institutions into a position which, although we trust not now dangerous, will certainly become so, except under the guidance of sound discretion in their future counsels, and will postpone indefinitely a return to specie payments, to the restoration of which our aim should be steadily directed, since whatever inducements any other institutions may have to render more probable the recovery of heavy loans

1841 by a general depreciation of the currency, the interests of this bank will be best promoted by maintaining the highest standard compatible with existing circumstances."

There were in addition other features of the act which rendered it peculiarly obnoxious to the bank. Its constitutionality was not beyond dispute, nor were the proffered immunities extended beyond exemption from penalties *theretofore* enacted.

Much of all that could be gained by compliance with its terms it was thought the bank would be allowed, at any rate, from necessity, to enjoy in common with the loaning banks. Besides, the directors were of opinion "that attempts to propitiate legislative power by pecuniary sacrifices are essentially unwise and dangerous, inasmuch as they invite new aggressions, which will be limited only by the final inability of the exhausted institutions to pay the price of further exemption."

Directors' Minutes, June 8, 1841.

Ibid., June 10, 1841.

A report embodying the views above set forth was presented to a meeting of the stockholders convened on June 10, 1841, and it was finally agreed by them that the bank should decline to accept the provisions of the act. A few of the other city banks adopted the same course, the wisdom of which was speedily justified.

Ibid., June 28, 1841.

So strong did the Bank of North America now feel that on June 28 it announced its readiness to pay all of its own notes in specie, on demand. In order, however, to avoid complications, it soon after resolved to receive no new accounts, either from banks or individuals, nor would it accept more than one thousand dollars in any one day on deposit from any of its former customers.

1841

By the beginning of the year 1842 the Legislature again became uneasy at the continued state of suspension, and requested the banks generally throughout the State to furnish information as to when they deemed resumption practicable.

1842

Directors' Minutes, January 20, 1842.

To this request the directors of the Bank of North America promptly replied that they had redeemed all their notes, except about $24,000, which they would pay on demand in specie; that they had few deposits which were not by express contract payable in current funds; that their outstanding loans were strictly on business paper, in small amounts; and that they were prepared to resume as soon as the currency was raised to the standard of gold and silver. In order to accomplish this result they ventured to suggest that the Legislature should take speedy steps to raise the credit of the Commonwealth, so that those banks which had portions of their capital locked up in State loan, might convert it at a reasonable rate, and thus meet their outstanding obligations. They recommended too, that some method should be adopted for withdrawing the notes issued under

Ibid., January 25, 1842.

1842 the provisions of the "Relief Act." Until these measures were accomplished any attempt to return to a specie basis they feared would prove abortive.

To these wise counsels the Legislature paid no heed. By an act approved March 12, 1842, immediate resumption was commanded on the part of every bank in the Commonwealth, without any provision being made for the payment of interest on the State loans or the retirement of the "relief" notes. As a consequence, great difficulty was experienced by many of the banks in complying with the legislative mandate. On March 18 the Bank of North America and eight other city banks returned to a specie basis. But almost every bank which had accepted the provisions of the "Relief Act" was obliged to postpone the period of its resumption, and it was not until more than a year after, when provision had been made to replenish the exhausted Treasury of the State, and to cancel the notes issued under the "Relief Act," that confidence and credit were in any degree restored to the mercantile and financial world.

The Bank of North America had suffered most severely during the period which has just been described. At the opening of the year 1842 the president communicated to the directors the fact that in his opinion the bank stood in a most dangerous state. It had, in fact, about four-fifths of its capital locked up in unavailable securities, and

consequently only about one-fifth in an actually
available shape. A persistent reduction of accommodation loans, and of the discount line for some
time again ensued as the surest means of restoring
strength to the institution.

As the year went on, however, the disastrous
effects of the late crisis became more and more
apparent. The actual assets of the bank had so
far depreciated in value, the prospects of realizing
any considerable part of the debt due from the
Bank of the United States were so doubtful and
remote, and the profits derived from the current
business were so scanty, that the directors did not
feel warranted in declaring any dividends to the
stockholders. The result was that many persons
were deprived of means absolutely essential to their
support. Application was, therefore, made to the
Legislature to pass an act authorizing the reduction of the capital, a measure which it was justly
supposed would enhance the market value of the
stock, promote confidence in the community at
large in the institution, and enable the directors to
declare reasonable dividends. The application was
successful. On March 24, 1843, an act to the desired effect became a law, cutting down the capital
stock of the bank to $750,000, and reducing the
par value of the shares to $300.

The effect was all that could be desired. In
January, 1842, the half-yearly dividend had been

1842

Directors'
Minutes,
January 6,
1842.

1843

Ibid., June
20 and 30,
1841; January 12,
1843.

Pamphlet
Laws, 168.

1843   passed, to the great distress of many of the stockholders. In July, 1842, a nominal dividend only of one cent per share had been declared in order to prevent a forfeiture of the charter. In January, 1843, the dividend was again passed. In July, 1843, but three months after the passage of the above-mentioned act, a half-yearly dividend of
1844   three per cent. was declared. In January, 1844, like action was taken, and by July of that year the directors felt warranted in distributing four per cent. on the capital to the stockholders.

Business meantime was rapidly reviving. Two years of prosperity availed to place the bank upon a footing so firm that it felt warranted in asking
1845   for a return of the capital to its old volume. This was effected by an act of the Legislature approved
Pamphlet Laws, 480.   April 16, 1845.

1846   In 1846 application was again made for the renewal of the charter. But this was not effected upon very favorable terms. The Legislature insisted upon inserting into the new act of incorporation a clause making the stockholders individually liable for the debts of the institution to an amount equal to the par value of their stock. Nor was this the only objectionable provision. If the bank should at any time appear to be in failing circumstances, a summary method was provided for winding up its affairs; and in the event of its assets falling below the amount of its

capital, the governor was authorized and required
to renew the charter, with a capital correspondingly reduced.

Another feature of this act was the reduction of the par value of the shares to $100 each, although their number was so enlarged as to represent the full capital of a million of dollars.

This act bore date April 8, 1846, and was accepted by the stockholders on January 11, 1847. By its terms the corporate existence of the bank was continued for ten years from the expiration of the former charter.

1846

Act. April 8, 1846. Pamphlet Laws, 1847, 20.

1847

Stockholders' Minutes, January 11, 1847.

CHAPTER VII.

1847-1882.

Erection of the present Banking-House in 1847—Renewal of the Charter in 1855—The Panic of 1857—Resignation of John Richardson from the Presidency in 1857—Election of James N. Dickson, and his Resignation in 1860—Election of Thomas Smith as President—The War of the Rebellion—Assistance afforded to the Government by the Bank from 1861 to 1864—Loyalty of the Bank—Its Reorganization as a National Bank in 1864—Retention of its Old Title without the usual Prefix "National"—Conclusion.

IN the year 1847 the old building, in which the Bank of North America had now transacted its business for upwards of sixty-five years, was at length deemed too inconvenient and too ruinous for further occupancy. It had, in fact, never been very well adapted to the purposes of the bank. As early as 1784 the directors had discussed the propriety of removing elsewhere, and upon one occasion the bank had by the merest accident escaped the perpetration of a robbery, which the fragile construction of its walls would have rendered easy.¹ It was, therefore, resolved to erect a new banking-house on the old site better suited to the requirements of the institution.²

The bank removed on June 11, 1847, to temporary quarters adjoining the Philadelphia Bank,

1847
Directors'
Minutes,
May 29,
1847.

---

¹ When Porter, the mail-robber, was arrested, tried, and sentenced to death for robbing the Reading mail, in December, 1829, he sent for James S. Smith, Esq., counsel for the bank, and confessed to him that a plan had been framed for robbing the bank, which would undoubtedly have been put in execution but for his arrest. The method in which this was to have been accomplished was substantially as follows:

A narrow alley ran northward from Chestnut Street, on the west side of the bank, which was at that time patrolled at night by a watchman employed by the bank. Porter and his confederates had, on some pretence, obtained access to the banking-house during business hours, and had discovered that the vault wherein the specie was kept was situate on the western side of the building, looking on this alley. They found, too, that owing to the miserable construction of the whole building, but one thickness of brick intervened between the alley and the vault. Having ascertained the distance of the vault from the front of the building, they had stepped a like distance in the alley, and had actually marked that part of the western wall constituting the back of the vault. Their plan was to seize and gag the bank watchman at night, to cut through the thin brick wall, and so possess themselves of the contents of the vault.

Porter refused to divulge who were his confederates, but so accurate was his knowledge as to the contents of the vault that collusion with some employé of the bank was suspected.

On hearing this story the directors, of course, at once took steps to have the western wall so strengthened as to preclude the possibility of another such attempt.

² The attention of the directors was forcibly directed to the ruinous state of the building by the sudden falling of two bricks from the wall into the president's room, during business hours, in the early part of 1847.

1848
Directors'
Minutes,
May 24, 1847.

Ibid., March
11, 1848.

1855

Act, April
8, 1846.
Pamphlet
Laws, 367.
Stockhold-
ers' Minutes,
June 11,
1855.

1857

Directors'
Minutes,
September 25
and 26, 1857.

Ibid., April
27, 1857.

then situate at the southwest corner of Fourth and Chestnut Streets, and there transacted business for exactly nine months. At the expiration of that time the new building, as it now stands, was ready for occupancy, and on March 11, 1848, its doors were opened to the public.

On April 26, 1855, the charter of the bank was again renewed for a period of twenty years, upon the terms of the act of 1846. The stockholders, without objection or difficulty, accepted the new charter at a meeting convened on June 11, 1855.

During the great panic of the year 1857 the Bank of North America was compelled again for a while, in common with the other banks of the country, to suspend the payment of specie. But the difficulty was only temporary. The suspension began on September 26, 1857, and resumption was effected by the following spring.

On April 27 of the same year John Richardson presented to the directors his resignation from the position of president, assigning as his reason the very close confinement necessitated by the duties of the office. The resignation did not, however, go into effect until the July following, when the directors took the opportunity to express their appreciation of his "soundness of judgment and promptness of action, his strict adherence to right principles, and his zealous, untiring devotion to the interests of the institution." "The whole of

PRESIDENT OF THE BANK OF NORTH AMERICA
1857-1860

THE BANK OF NORTH AMERICA. 113

the long period during which he was in office," they declared, "had been marked by the most uninterrupted harmony and mutual respect, and, on the part of the board, by the highest regard for the excellent qualities of Mr. Richardson as an officer and a man."

1857

Directors' Minutes, July 16, 1857.

On July 16, 1857, James N. Dickson was elected to fill the vacancy, but his term of office extended over little more than three years. On August 9, 1860, he presented his resignation, and on the 20th of the same month Thomas Smith was chosen as his successor. Mr. Smith has now been in office for upwards of twenty-one years, a longer period than any previous president of the institution.

Ibid.

1860

Ibid., August 9, 1860.

Ibid., August 20, 1860.

When the War of the Rebellion broke out, the Bank of North America was among the first of the banking institutions of the country to declare its unabated confidence in and regard for the National Government. Loyal alike from inclination and from a profound sentiment of gratitude to the power that had first brought it into existence, it hastened to take measures to aid in the preservation of the integrity of that National Union which it had done so much to promote.

1861

On April 22, 1861, the directors, by a unanimous vote, appropriated the sum of $5000 to the Committee of Public Safety, in order to provide for the defence of the city and the preservation of the public peace.

Ibid., April 22, 1861.

1861

Directors' Minutes, May 23, 1861.

In the following May it agreed, in common with the other banks of the city, to subscribe for its pro rata share of United States Treasury notes. In July it loaned to the United States directly the sum of $100,000 in coin for sixty days, at six per cent. interest, agreeing that the advance might be returned either in kind or in 7.30 notes. In August it subscribed $400,000 for these same 7.30 notes, and in September took its pro rata share of $50,000,000 on the same security. In November it subscribed for its pro rata share of $5,000,000 in United States six per cent. bonds.

Ibid., July 23, 1861.

Ibid., August 17, 1861.

Ibid., September 25, 1861.

Ibid., November 19, 1861.

Ibid., December 31, 1861.

On December 31, 1861, the bank was forced, in common with the other banking institutions of the country, to suspend the payment of specie. But this occurrence by no means diminished either its ability or its disposition to aid the national cause.

1862

On February 28, 1862, it made an advance to the Treasury of $300,000 at five per cent. interest, on condition that the amount should be returned on ten days' notice, in kind.

Ibid., February 28, 1862.

Ibid., July 3, 1862.

On July 3 $300,000 more were invested in United States securities. On July 28, at a meeting of the directors, the following resolutions were unanimously adopted:

Whereas, This bank was instituted in 1781 to aid the colonies in their struggle for independence;

And whereas, It has ever since prospered under the Government it assisted in creating;

And whereas, In carrying out the policy of making contributions to such objects only as are within its legitimate sphere, the stability of the Government is most essential to the interests of the stockholders; it is, therefore,

Resolved, That the sum of five thousand dollars be contributed by the bank, and disposed of in such manner as the president may deem most expedient to assist the Government in maintaining its integrity.

1862

Directors' Minutes, July 28, 1862.

During the year 1863 the same policy was pursued. During the month of May the sum of $600,000 was invested in United States twelve months' certificates. In July the sum of $40,000 was loaned to the State to aid in the payment of its troops. In the same month half a million more of United States twelve months' certificates were taken, and in November the sum of $100,000 was invested in the United States 7.30 notes.

1863

Ibid., May 18 and 28, 1863.

Ibid., July 27, 1863.

Ibid.

Ibid., November 2, 1863.

On January 14, 1864, the president was authorized to advance at proper times still further sums on the United States twelve months' certificates, but the amount of these securities held never exceeded at any one time a million and a half of dollars. Nor was the mere advancing of money to the Government the only method which the bank took of testifying its patriotism. It advanced at various times to individuals no less than two millions of dollars on the deposit of United States securities as

1864

Ibid., January 14, 1864.

collateral. And in order to stimulate the employés to volunteer for the national defence, it was resolved by the directors that the salaries of all clerks who might be absent on the service of the State, or of the United States, should be continued as though no interruption to their daily labors had taken place.

In October, 1864, a correspondence was opened with the Comptroller of the Currency in Washington, looking to the reorganization of the institution as a national bank, under the "National Currency Act," passed by Congress June 3, 1864. A step more in keeping with the traditions and history of the bank it would be hard to conceive. Created by Congress, and fostered under national auspices, it was only by the force of circumstances, and the unfortunate prevalence of the State Rights' feeling, that it had been forced into the position of a State institution. It had already given ample evidence of its loyalty to the national cause. It had advanced four and a half millions of dollars, or four and a half times the amount of its capital stock, on United States securities, and it now embraced the opportunity of resuming its former intimate relations with the National Government. Much feeling, however, prevailed, both among the directors and the stockholders, against any change in the old corporate title of "The Bank of North America." It was felt by them that the addition

Marginalia:
1864

Directors' Minutes, May 26, 1864.

See Appendix.

Letter, Thomas Smith, Esq., President of the Bank, to Hon. Hugh McCulloch, Comptroller, etc., November 1, 1864. See Appendix.

of the word "National," as was customary on becoming a national bank, was, in the case of the Bank of North America, both unnecessary and ill-advised. Its original national name conferred upon it by Congress, as well as its original national character, had always been, and still continue to be, matters of great pride to those interested in the institution. These views were presented at great length to the Comptroller of the Currency in a letter from the president of the bank, but failed at first to meet with his approbation.

1864

See Appendix.

On November 14, 1864, the stockholders met to consider the propriety of becoming a national bank. The requisite two-thirds vote approving the change was readily obtained. It was resolved that the State charter should be surrendered, that new articles of association should be executed, that the bank should reorganize under the provisions of the act of Congress, and that the assets of the old corporation should be transferred to the possession of the new.

Stockholders' Minutes, November 14, 1864.

These changes were at once effected. In November a committee of the directors was despatched to Washington to deposit the necessary securities, and immediately after the bank began business in its new national character.

The result of the correspondence with the Comptroller of the Treasury, already described, was to induce him at length to consent to the retention by

1864	the bank of its old corporate title, without the prefix "National." In this action he was largely influenced by a memorial signed by the presidents of most of the other Philadelphia banks, expressing their entire approval of the scheme for leaving the title unchanged. It is believed that this is the only instance in the country where a similar permission was extended.
Directors' Minutes, November 23, 1864.	
1882	A century has now passed away since the Bank of North America first opened its doors. It has lived to see a weak confederation of States grow into a great and prosperous nation. It has witnessed periods of unbounded commercial prosperity and others of most deplorable distress. But throughout all it has never failed, by the maintenance of a sound financial policy, to command the respect and esteem of the mercantile and financial world. As long as it retains these it may look forward with well-grounded confidence to a future of undiminished prosperity and usefulness.

PRESIDENT OF THE BANK OF NORTH AMERICA
ELECTED IN 1860

APPENDIX.

I.

LIST OF THE PRESIDENTS, CASHIERS, AND DIRECTORS OF THE BANK OF NORTH AMERICA FROM ITS FOUNDATION TO THE PRESENT TIME.

PRESIDENTS.

Name.	Elected.	Term of Office ended.
Thomas Willing	November 2, 1781	Resigned Jan. 9, 1792.
John Nixon	January 10, 1792	Died December 31, 1808.
John Morton	January 10, 1809	Resigned Jan. 15, 1822.
Henry Nixon	January 15, 1822	Died August 18, 1840.
John Richardson	September 3, 1840	Resigned July 16, 1857.
James N. Dickson	July 16, 1857	Resigned Aug. 9, 1860.
Thomas Smith	August 20, 1860	

CASHIERS.

Name.	Elected.	Term of Office ended.
Tench Francis	November 26, 1781	January 12, 1792.
Richard Wells	January 12, 1792	Resigned Jan. 30, 1800.
Henry Drinker, Jr.	January 30, 1800	Died October 19, 1822.
Henry Hollingsworth	October 30, 1822	Resigned Aug. 31, 1840.
James Correy	September 17, 1840	Resigned Feb. 20, 1843.
John Hockley	March 6, 1843	Resigned May 1, 1869.
John H. Watt	May 1, 1869	

120   A HISTORY OF

DIRECTORS.

Name.	Elected.	Term of Office ended.
Thomas Willing	November 1, 1781	January 9, 1792.
Thomas Fitzsimons	November 1, 1781	January 10, 1803.
John Maxwell Nesbitt	November 1, 1781	January 9, 1792.
James Wilson	November 1, 1781	January 12, 1784.
Henry Hill	November 1, 1781	January 9, 1792.
Samuel Osgood	November 1, 1781	January 12, 1784.
Cadwalader Morris	November 1, 1781	April 25, 1786.
Samuel Inglis	November 1, 1781	January 12, 1784.
Samuel Meredith	November 1, 1781	January 12, 1784.
William Bingham	November 1, 1781	January 12, 1784.
Timothy Matlack	November 1, 1781	November 4, 1782.
Andrew Caldwell	November 1, 1781	January 10, 1791.
George Haynes	November 4, 1782	January 12, 1784.
Mordecai Lewis	January 12, 1784	January 13, 1800.
John Ross	January 12, 1784	January 9, 1792.
John Nixon	January 12, 1784	Resigned Dec. 24, 1808.
Samuel Powel	January 12, 1784	January 9, 1792.
Richard Bache	January 12, 1784	January 9, 1792.
Josiah Hewes	January 12, 1784	Resigned Jan. 10, 1805.
Andrew Tybout	May 29, 1786	January 9, 1792.
Joseph Swift	January 10, 1791	January 9, 1804.
George Latimer	January 9, 1792	Died June 13, 1825.
Benjamin Fuller	January 9, 1792	January 13, 1800.
Miers Fisher	January 9, 1792	January 13, 1800.
John Swanwick	January 9, 1792	January 14, 1793.
John Morton	January 9, 1792	Died April 23, 1828.
Robert Waln	January 9, 1792	January 10, 1820.
William T. Smith	January 9, 1792	Died February, 1812.
Richard Rundle	January 14, 1793	January 13, 1800.
Thomas Murgatroyd	January 13, 1800	January 13, 1801.
Gideon Hill Wells	January 13, 1800	January 10, 1803.
Daniel Smith	January 13, 1800	January 7, 1833.
Anthony Morris	January 13, 1800	January 11, 1808.
Jacob Downing	January 13, 1801	January 12, 1818.
James Smith, Jr.	January 10, 1803	January 14, 1811.

DIRECTORS.—Continued.

Name.	Elected.	Term of Office ended.
Joseph S. Lewis	January 9, 1804	January 12, 1818.
James Read	January 14, 1805	January 13, 1823.
William Waln	January 14, 1805	January 10, 1820.
Timothy Paxson	January 11, 1808	Died April 21, 1839.
Henry Nixon	January 9, 1809	Died August 18, 1840.
Benjamin R. Morgan	January 14, 1811	Resigned August, 1821.
Abraham Kintzing	April 1, 1812	January 11, 1819.
George Fox	January 12, 1818	Died September 9, 1828.
George McCallmont	January 12, 1818	January 7, 1833.
Charles McAlester	January 11, 1819	Died August 29, 1832.
Joseph Peace	January 10, 1820	Died April, 1826.
Jacob S. Waln	January 10, 1820	Resigned June 23, 1828.
George Roberts	September 7, 1821	January 10, 1825.
Edward Penington	January 13, 1823	January 10, 1825.
Alexander Elmslie	January 10, 1825	January 12, 1829.
Richard Randolph	January 10, 1825	Resigned April 7, 1828.
Newman Cope	January 9, 1826	Resigned March 6, 1826.
Coleman Fisher	June 5, 1826	Resigned Oct. 9, 1843.
Charles H. Baker	June 5, 1826	Resigned Dec. 21, 1829.
Furman Leaming	July 24, 1828	Died March, 1832.
Samuel Hollingsworth	July 24, 1828	Resigned Jan. 14, 1833.
John Clement Stocker	July 24, 1828	Died July 29, 1833.
John M. Attwood	January 5, 1829	Resigned Oct. 9, 1843.
Benjamin W. Richards	April 2, 1829	Resigned Jan. 18, 1830.
John Miller, Jr.	January 5, 1830	Died May 12, 1836.
David Lewis, Jr.	April 26, 1830	Resigned ——, 1840.
George Handy	April 30, 1832	Resigned Oct. 27, 1834.
" "	May 26, 1836	Resigned Nov. 26, 1838.
William W. Keen	November 29, 1832	Resigned Oct. 16, 1843.
" "	March 17, 1845	Resigned Mar. 20, 1848.
" "	January 6, 1851	January 2, 1854.
" "	January 2, 1855	January 31, 1859.
John Richardson	January 7, 1833	January 31, 1859.
Richard S. Smith	January 7, 1833	Resigned April 17, 1834.
Joseph P. Homer	October 31, 1833	Resigned Aug. 8, 1842.

DIRECTORS.—Continued.

Name.	Elected.	Term of Office ended.
Charles Bird	October 31, 1833	Resigned Oct. 27, 1834.
Jacob Lex	October 6, 1834	Resigned Nov. 22, 1838.
Edward Yarnall	November 24, 1834	Resigned Oct. 19, 1843.
" "	January 8, 1850	January 3, 1853.
" "	January 2, 1854	January 5, 1857.
Thomas Robins	November 27, 1834	Resigned Jan. 30, 1843.
" "	July 15, 1844	Resigned July 12, 1847.
" "	September 4, 1848	Resigned Sept. 4, 1851.
Thomas Allibone	December 3, 1838	January 1, 1844.
" "	March 19, 1846	Resigned Mar. 19, 1849.
John B. Budd	December 3, 1838	January 1, 1844.
" "	January 6, 1845	January 3, 1848.
" "	January 1, 1849	January 6, 1852.
" "	January 3, 1853	January 7, 1856.
A. J. Lewis	September 21, 1840	January 1, 1844.
" "	October 26, 1846	Resigned Oct. 25, 1849.
" "	November 17, 1851	Resigned Nov. 22, 1854.
" "	January 7, 1856	January 2, 1860.
" "	January 7, 1861	January 4, 1864.
" "	January 10, 1865	January 14, 1868.
" "	January 12, 1869	January 10, 1872.
" "	January 14, 1873	January 11, 1876.
" "	January 9, 1877	Died May, 1877.
James N. Dickson	September 21, 1840	January 1, 1844.
" "	January 3, 1848	January 6, 1851.
" "	October 18, 1852	January 7, 1856.
" "	January 5, 1857	January 5, 1863.
Thomas M. Smith	January 5, 1841	January 1, 1844.
" "	January 6, 1845	January 3, 1848.
" "	October 15, 1849	January 3, 1853.
" "	January 2, 1854	January 5, 1857.
James C. Hand	October 31, 1842	Resigned Oct. 30, 1845.
" "	January 1, 1849	January 6, 1852.
" "	January 2, 1855	January 2, 1860.
" "	January 7, 1861	January 4, 1864.

THE BANK OF NORTH AMERICA. 123

DIRECTORS.—Continued.

Name.	Elected.	Term of Office ended.
James C. Hand	January 10, 1865	January 14, 1868.
" "	January 12, 1869	January 10, 1872.
" "	January 14, 1873	January 11, 1876.
" "	January 9, 1877	January 13, 1880.
" "	January 11, 1881	
Stephen Baldwin	June 15, 1843	Resigned Oct. 1, 1846.
" "	January 3, 1848	January 6, 1851.
Morris L. Hallowell	October 12, 1843	Resigned Oct. 8, 1846.
" "	October 15, 1849	Resigned Oct. 11, 1852.
" "	January 2, 1854	January 5, 1857.
" "	January 2, 1860	January 7, 1862.
John Gregg	October 19, 1843	Resigned Oct. 1, 1846.
" "	January 8, 1850	Resigned Sept. 1, 1851.
Henry Sloan	October 19, 1843	Resigned Oct. 12, 1846.
" "	January 3, 1848	January 6, 1851.
" "	January 6, 1852	January 1, 1855.
" "	January 7, 1856	Resigned Dec. 16, 1858.
" "	January 10, 1871	January 14, 1873.
William S. Boyd	October 27, 1843	Resigned Feb. 12, 1846.
Thomas T. Lea	January 1, 1844	January 5, 1847.
" "	November 5, 1849	January 3, 1853.
" "	January 2, 1854	January 5, 1857.
John Dickson	January 1, 1844	Resigned Jan. 2, 1845.
Benjamin T. Curtis	November 10, 1845	Resigned Nov. 20, 1848.
" "	January 6, 1852	January 1, 1855.
Hugh Elliott	October 12, 1846	Resigned Oct. 11, 1849.
" "	January 3, 1853	Resigned May 16, 1853.
John H. Brown	October 12, 1846	Resigned Oct. 18, 1849.
" "	January 6, 1851	January 2, 1854.
" "	January 2, 1855	January 1, 1860.
" "	January 7, 1861	January 4, 1864.
" "	January 10, 1865	January 14, 1868.
" "	January 12, 1869	January 10, 1872.
" "	January 14, 1873	January 11, 1876.
" "	January 9, 1877	January 13, 1880.

DIRECTORS.—Continued.

Name.	Elected.	Term of Office ended.
John H. Brown	January 11, 1881	
Jacob P. Jones	October 12, 1846	Resigned Oct. 15, 1849.
" "	November 17, 1851	Resigned Nov. 20, 1854.
" "	January 7, 1856	January 2, 1860.
" "	January 5, 1863	January 9, 1866.
" "	January 8, 1867	January 12, 1870.
" "	January 10, 1871	January 13, 1874.
" "	January 12, 1875	January 10, 1878.
" "	January 14, 1879	
Paul W. Newhall	January 5, 1847	Resigned Feb. 17, 1848.
Thomas Smith	January 6, 1851	January 2, 1854.
" "	January 2, 1855	Resigned Feb. 10, 1859.
" "	January 2, 1860	
Lewis Audenried	January 3, 1853	January 7, 1856.
" "	January 5, 1857	January 7, 1861.
" "	January 6, 1862	January 10, 1865.
" "	January 9, 1866	January 12, 1869.
" "	January 12, 1870	January 14, 1873.
Wm. G. Audenried	January 13, 1874	January 9, 1877.
" "	January 8, 1878	January 11, 1881.
William L. Rehn	January 5, 1857	January 7, 1861.
" "	January 6, 1862	January 10, 1865.
" "	January 9, 1866	January 12, 1869.
" "	January 12, 1870	January 14, 1873.
" "	January 13, 1874	Resigned Jan. 15, 1874.
John H. Irwin	January 5, 1857	January 7, 1861.
" "	January 6, 1862	January 10, 1865.
" "	January 9, 1866	January 12, 1869.
" "	January 12, 1870	Died March, 1870.
John M. Whitall	January 31, 1859	January 6, 1862.
" "	January 5, 1863	January 9, 1866.
" "	January 14, 1868	January 10, 1871.
Charles S. Lewis	January 31, 1859	January 6, 1862.
" "	January 5, 1863	January 9, 1866.
" "	January 8, 1867	January 12, 1870.

DIRECTORS—Continued.

Name.	Elected.	Term of Office Ended.
Charles S. Lewis	January 10, 1871	January 13, 1874.
" "	January 12, 1875	January 10, 1878.
" "	January 14, 1879	
Henry Lewis	January 31, 1859	January 6, 1862.
" "	January 5, 1863	January 9, 1866.
" "	January 8, 1867	January 12, 1870.
" "	January 10, 1871	January 13, 1874.
" "	January 12, 1875	January 10, 1878.
" "	January 14, 1879	
David Scull	January 2, 1860	January 5, 1863.
" "	January 4, 1864	January 8, 1867.
" "	January 14, 1868	January 10, 1871.
" "	January 10, 1872	January 13, 1875.
Israel Morris	January 2, 1860	January 5, 1863.
" "	January 10, 1865	January 14, 1868.
" "	January 12, 1869	January 10, 1872.
" "	January 13, 1874	January 9, 1877.
" "	January 8, 1878	January 11, 1881.
James O. Pease	January 2, 1860	January 5, 1863.
" "	January 4, 1864	January 8, 1867.
Charles Vezin	January 6, 1862	January 10, 1865.
" "	January 9, 1866	January 12, 1869.
John P. Levy	January 4, 1864	January 8, 1867.
Lemuel Coffin	January 14, 1868	January 10, 1871.
" "	January 10, 1872	January 13, 1875.
" "	January 11, 1876	January 14, 1879.
" "	January 13, 1880	
William B. Kempton	January 14, 1868	January 10, 1871.
" "	January 10, 1872	January 13, 1875.
" "	January 11, 1876	January 14, 1879.
" "	January 13, 1880	
John H. Michener	January 10, 1871	January 13, 1874.
" "	January 12, 1875	January 10, 1878.
" "	January 14, 1879	
Henry Winsor	January 10, 1872	January 13, 1875.

DIRECTORS.—Continued.

Name.	Elected.	Term of Office ended.
Henry Winsor	January 11, 1876	January 14, 1879.
" "	January 13, 1880	
Clement A. Griscom	January 3, 1874	January 9, 1877.
" "	January 8, 1878	January 11, 1881.
George W. Fiss	February 12, 1874	January 9, 1877.
" "	January 8, 1878	January 11, 1881.
Theodore C. Search	January 9, 1877	January 10, 1878.
" "	January 11, 1881	
William Simpson, Jr.	May 11, 1877	January 13, 1880.
" "	January 11, 1881	
R. H. Downing	January 8, 1878	January 14, 1879.

II.

On the 17th day of May, 1781, the following Plan was submitted to the consideration of the United States in Congress assembled:

PLAN FOR ESTABLISHING A NATIONAL BANK FOR THE UNITED STATES OF NORTH AMERICA.

1st. That a Subscription be opened for four hundred thousand dollars, in Shares of Four hundred dollars each, to be paid in Gold or Silver.

2d. That the subscription be paid into the Hands of George Clymer and John Nixon, Esqrs., or their agents.

3d. That every subscriber of less than five shares pay the whole sum on the day of his subscription.

4th. That every subscriber of Five Shares, or upwards, pay one-half the Sum on the day of his subscription, and the other half within three months of that day.

5th. That every holder of a share shall be entitled to a vote by himself, his agent, or proxy, properly appointed, at all Elections of Directors, and that he have as many votes as he hold shares, and that every Subscriber may Sell or Transfer his Share or Shares at his pleasure, the Transfer being made in the Bank Books, in presence and with the approbation of the proprietor or his Lawful Attorney, the purchaser then to become entitled to the right of Voting, &c.

6th. That there be Twelve Directors chosen from among

those entitled to vote, who, at their first meeting, shall choose one as President.

7th. That there be a meeting of the Directors Quarterly, for the purpose of Regulating the affairs of the Bank, and seven of the Directors to make a Board, and that the Board have power to adjourn from time to time.

8th. That the Board of Directors determine the manner of doing Business, and the Rules and Forms to be pursued, appoint the various Officers which they may find necessary, and dispose of the Money and Credit of the Bank for the Interest and Benefit of the proprietors, and make from time to time such Dividends, out of the Profits, as they may think proper.

9th. That the Board be empowered from time to time to open new subscriptions, for the purpose of increasing the Capital of the Bank, on such terms and conditions as they shall think proper.

10th. That the Board shall at every quarterly meeting Choose two Directors, to inspect and control the Business of the Bank, for the ensuing three months.

11th. That the Inspectors so chosen shall, on the evening of every day, Sundays excepted, deliver to the Superintendent of the Finances of America a state of the Cash account, and of the Notes issued and Received.

12th. That the Bank Notes, payable on demand, shall by Law be made receivable for the Duties and Taxes of every State in the Union, and from the Respective States, by the Treasury of the United States, as specie.

13th. That the Superintendent of the Finances of America shall have a right, at all times, to examine into the affairs of the Bank, and for that purpose shall have access to all the Books and Papers.

14th. That any Director or Officer of the Bank, who shall

convert any of the property, monies, or credits thereof, to his own use, or shall in any other way be guilty of Fraud or Embezzlement, shall forfeit all his share or stock to the Company.

15th. That Laws shall be passed making it felony without Benefit of Clergy to commit such Fraud or Embezzlement.

16th. That the Subscribers shall be Incorporated under the Name of "The President, Directors, and Company of the Bank of North America."

17th. That none of the Directors shall be entitled to any pecuniary advantage for his attendance on the duties of his office as Director, or President, or Inspector, unless an alteration, in this respect, shall hereafter be made by the consent of a majority of the Stockholders, at a general election.

18th. That as soon as the Subscription shall be filled, George Clymer and John Nixon, Esqrs., shall publish a list of the names and sums respectively subscribed, with the place of abode of the Subscribers, and appoint a day for the choice of Directors, to whom, when chosen, they shall deliver over the Money by them received.

III.

By the United States in Congress assembled, December 31, 1781.

AN ORDINANCE TO INCORPORATE THE SUBSCRIBERS TO THE BANK OF NORTH AMERICA.

Whereas, Congress, on the twenty-sixth day of May last, did, from a conviction of the support which the finances of the United States would receive from the establishment of a national bank, approve a plan for such an institution, submitted to their consideration by Robert Morris, Esq., and now lodged among the archives of Congress, and did engage to promote the same by the most effectual means; and whereas, the subscription thereto is now filled from an expectation of a charter of incorporation from Congress, the directors and president are chosen, and application hath been made to Congress by the said president and directors for an act of incorporation; and whereas, the exigencies of the United States render it indispensably necessary that such an act be immediately passed.

Be it therefore ordained, and it is hereby ordained, by the United States in Congress assembled, that those who are, and those who shall become, subscribers to the said bank, be, and forever after shall be, a corporation and body politic to all intents and purposes, by the name and style of THE PRESIDENT, DIRECTORS, AND COMPANY OF THE BANK OF NORTH AMERICA.

And be it further ordained, that the said corporation are hereby declared and made able and capable in law, to have, purchase, receive, possess, enjoy, and retain lands, rents, tenements, hereditaments, goods, chattels, and effects, of what kind, nature, or quality soever, to the amount of ten millions of Spanish silver milled dollars, and no more; and also to sell, grant, demise, alien, or dispose of the same lands, rents, tenements, hereditaments, goods, chattels, and effects.

And be it further ordained, that the said corporation be, and shall be, forever hereafter, able and capable, in law, to sue and be sued, plead and be impleaded, answer and be answered unto, defend and be defended, in courts of record, or any other place whatsoever, and to do and execute all and singular other matters and things that to them shall or may appertain to do.

And be it further ordained, that for the well governing of the said corporation, and the ordering of their affairs, they shall have such officers as they shall hereafter direct or appoint, provided, nevertheless, that twelve directors, one of whom shall be the president of the corporation, be of the number of their officers.

And be it further ordained, that Thomas Willing be the present president, and the said Thomas Willing and Thomas Fitzsimons, John Maxwell Nesbitt, James Wilson, Henry Hill, Samuel Osgood, Cadwalader Morris, Andrew Caldwell, Samuel Inglis, Samuel Meredith, William Bingham, and Timothy Matlack be the present directors of the said corporation, and shall so continue until another president and other directors shall be chosen according to the laws and regulations of the said corporation.

And be it further ordained, that the president and directors of the said corporation shall be capable of exercising such power for the well governing and ordering of the affairs of the said corporation, and of holding such occasional meetings for that purpose, as shall be described, fixed, and determined by the laws, regulations, and ordinances of the said corporation.

And be it further ordained, that said corporation may make, ordain, establish, and put in execution such laws, ordinances, and regulations as shall seem necessary and convenient to the government of the said corporation. Provided always, that nothing hereinbefore contained shall be construed to authorize the said corporation to exercise any powers in any of the United States repugnant to the laws or constitution of such State.

And be it further ordained, that the said corporation shall have full power and authority to make, have, and use a common seal, with such device and inscription as they think proper, and the same to break, alter, and renew at their pleasure.

And be it further ordained, that this ordinance shall be construed and taken most favorably and beneficially for the said corporation.

IV.

ALPHABETICAL LIST OF THE FIRST SUBSCRIBERS TO THE BANK OF NORTH AMERICA, TRANSCRIBED FROM THE ORIGINAL SUBSCRIPTION-PAPER, 1781, 1782, 1783.

This subscription was for 1000 shares at 400 dollars each.

APPLETON, NATHANIEL	1	CARTER, JOHN	98
BARGE, JACOB	1	COXE, TENCH	4
BARCLAY, JOHN	2	COX, JAMES	8
BINGHAM, W^m.	95	CALDWELL, JANE	1
BINGHAM, ANN	5	DUNLAP, JOHN	2
BINGHAM, MARY	7	DONNALDSON, JOHN	3
BRIDGES, ROB'T	1	DAVIDSON, JOHN	1
BROWN, MARY	1	DENNING, W^m.	5
BELL, DANIEL	1	DAVIS, CALEB	1
BRADFORD, JOHN	1	DECATUR, STEPHEN	3
BRECK, SAM'L	2	DICKINSON, PHILEMON	13
BAKER, JOHN	3	DYER, SARAH	1
BENEZET, PHILIP	1	DELAPLAINE, SAM^l.	1
BACHE, RICHARD	10	EDDY, GEORGE	1
BEAVAN, W^m.	2	EMLEN, GEORGE	2
BROWN, JOHN	18	FITZSIMONS, THOS.	2
BARTRAM, ANN	2	FULLER, BENJ.	10
BELL, W^m.	5	FROMBERGER, JOHN	1
CONYNGHAM, D. HAYFIELD	1	FRANKLIN, JOHN	12
CLYMER, GEORGE	7	FRANCIS, TENCH	4
CARSON, JOSEPH	1	FOX, JOS. M.	1
CALDWELL, AND^w. & JAMES	4	GURNEY, FRANCIS	1
CRAWFORD, JAMES	1	HAYNES, GEO.	2
CRAIG, JAMES, JUN^r.	1	HILL, HENRY	5
CODMAN & SMITH	1	HOLKER, JOHN	5

17

Hillegas, Michael	1	Nichols, Francis	1
Hatch, Crowell	2	Nathan, Simon	1
Hockley, W^m. B.	7	Osgood, Sam'l	1
Hazlehurst, Isaac	3	Ozeas, Peter	1
Hewes, Josiah	2	Otis, Samuel	2
Hare, Rob't	1	Pettit, Charles	1
Hopkinson, Francis	5	Penrose, Thos.	4
Inglis, Samuel, & Co.	4	Paca, W^m.	2
Irvin, Thos.	1	Peters, Rich^d.	2
Jones, John Paul	25	Parker, Daniel	1
Jarvis & Russell	5	Parsons, Theophilus	1
Kidd, John	4	Powel, Sam'l	23
Low, Nicholas	1	Poelnitz, Baron	12
Lardner, John	1	Price, Edwd.	1
Langdon, John	5	Pringle, John	3
Luzerne, Chevalier De La	1	Ross, John	5
Lieper, Thomas	2	Russell, Thos.	5
Lowell, John	1	Robertson, Alex^r.	10
Lewis, Mordecai	5	Rush, Benj.	1
Mease, John	1	Read, Jas.	7
Morris, Robert	98	Shiel, Hugh	1
Meade, George	3	Semple, W^m.	1
Mitchell, John	2	Swanwick, John	71
Mitchell, Henry	2	Smith, Charles	3
McClenachan, Blair	11	Salomon, Haym	2
Morris, Cadwalader	1	Shoemaker, Thomas	2
Meredith, Sam'l	7	Shippen, Edwd.	10
Mease & Caldwell	2	Stuart, Jas.	1
Morris, Gouverneur	1	Smith, W^m.	50
Moses, Isaac	1	Simpson, George	1
Moore, Philip	1	Strettell, Frances	1
Morris, Hannah	1	Stamper, John	4
Milligan, Ja^s.	3	Stewart and Totten	1
Marbois, Barbé de	1	Swyler, Jacob L.	1
McMurtrie, W^m.	12	Tilghman, Tench	1
Morris, W^m.	1	Tilghman, Jas.	13
Matlack, Timothy	1	Turnbull, W^m.	2
Nesbitt, John M.	1	Timmons, Dean	2
Nixon, John	5	Tracy, Nathl.	5

Totten, Rob't	1	Wendal, Oliver	1
Vanribber, Ab. & Jn°.	2	Wetmore, W^m.	1
Vaughan, John	4	Wadsworth, Jeremiah	104
Wilcocks, John	2	Winey, Jacob	3
Wilson, James	5	Whiteside, Peter	5
Wilcox, Mark	1	Wilson, John	2
Willing, Thomas	11	Wickersham, Amos	1
Willing, Charles	6		
Willing, Abby	2		1000
White, W^m.	1		

Of the above shares, the United States at first paid for 633, and the Bank, by special bargain, lent them the whole Money immediately, but, it not being convenient for the Financier to repay the money when wanted by the Bank, He reconveyed the said Shares, and they were bought up by some of the foregoing Subscribers.

N.B.—The first Subscription was thus completed on the 25th of July, 1783.

Thos. Willing, President.

V.

SECOND SUBSCRIPTION TO THE NATIONAL BANK, 1784.

At a general election, held at the bank January 12, 1784, a proposal was laid before the stockholders for opening a new subscription to enlarge the capital stock of the bank, upon which it was unanimously resolved

That a subscription shall be opened at the bank on the first day of February next, and continue until one thousand additional shares shall be subscribed.

That the price of each new share shall be five hundred dollars, and the amount of such shares shall be added to the present capital of the bank, so as to form one common stock, which shall be the property of the several stockholders, in proportion to the number of their respective shares, and without regard to the sum paid for such shares at the time of the subscription, and that in every case the money shall be paid at the time of subscribing.

Wherefore, we, the subscribers, having read the above resolution for increasing the capital stock of the bank, approving, confirming, and hereby agreeing to the same, we sign our names, and opposite thereto affix the number of shares for which we subscribe, having made and further agreeing to make payment according to the conditions above specified.

At the above general election the stockholders assigned to

THE BANK OF NORTH AMERICA. 137

THOMAS WILLING, President	Four shares.
JACOB BARGE	One share.
J. SWANWICK, on behalf of His Excellency P. J. VAN BERCKEL	Fifty shares.
J. SWANWICK	Thirty shares.
WILLING, MORRIS, & SWANWICK	Seventy shares.
DE HEYDER, VEYDT & Co., by HAYM SALOMON	Ten shares.
TENCH FRANCIS, on behalf of JOHN KIDD	Three shares.
WILLING, MORRIS, & SWANWICK	Nineteen shares.
CLEMENT BIDDLE & Co.	Three shares.
THOMAS LOWREY	One share.
ELEAZER OSWALD	One share.
ABRAM MARKOE	Four shares.
WILLIAM VAUGHAN, by JOHN VAUGHAN	One share.
JOHN DARBY, by D.	Four shares.
BENJAMIN FULLER	Ten shares.
TENCH FRANCIS, on behalf of WILLIAM BULL, ESQ.	One share.
RICHARD MASON	Two shares.
MILLER & ABERCROMBIE	One share.
SPENCER & MARACHE	Two shares.
HENRY PRATT	One share.
JOHN ROSS, for BARBÉ DE MARBOIS, ESQ.	Six shares.
JOHN ROSS	Ninety-four shares.
JAMES HOOD	Two shares.
NIXON & CLARKSON	One share.
SAMUEL COATES	One share.
NATHAN SELLERS	One share.
DAVID SELLERS	One share.
W. BARTON & Co.	One share.
CADWALADER MORRIS, for HANNAH MORRIS	One share.
CADWALADER MORRIS, for HANNAH MORRIS	One share.
SAMUEL JACKSON	One share.
NATHAN FALCONER	Two shares.
CORNELIUS BARNES	Two shares.
WILLIAM NICHOLS	Two shares.
SAMUEL POWEL	Twelve shares.
PETER LOHRA	One share.
GEORGE MEADE	Five shares.
SAMUEL POWEL	Two shares.

GEORGE MEADE, for FRANCES and ANNA MARIA CLIFTON	One share.
GEORGE MEADE, for CHARLOTTE PRETTEJOHN	One share.
GEORGE MEADE, for HENRIETTA CONSTANTIA MEADE	Three shares.
JOSEPH HARRISON	Two shares.
ROBERT MORRIS, by JAMES REES	Six shares.
Doctor JOHN BAKER	One share.
ISAAC VANBIBBER, by THOMAS WILLING	One share.
REED & FORDE	One share.
WILLIAM CONSTABLE, for SAMUEL FLEMING	Fifty shares.
JOHN FIELD	Two shares.
THOMAS PENROSE	Two shares.
WILLIAM RUIBEL	Two shares.
LAMB & CHECKLEY	Two shares.
JOHN WILCOCKS	Two shares.
ANDREW DOZ, for ABRAHAM WAYNE	One share.
JOHN BROWN & SONS	One share.
CONYNGHAM, NESBITT & Co., for D. H. CONYNGHAM	One share.
CONYNGHAM, NESBITT & Co., for J. M. NESBITT	One share.
KUHN & RISBERG	Two shares.
WILLIAM TILTON	Two shares.
MORDECAI LEWIS & Co.	Two shares.
EVAN EVANS, for MARY EVANS	One share.
JOHN BROWN	Twenty-two shares.
HAYM SALOMON	Two shares.
WILLIAM B. HOCKLEY, for the six minor children of my deceased sister.	Three shares.
GEORGE EDDY	Two shares.
WILLIAM CONSTABLE	Four shares.
JOHN and ROBERT MORTON	Two shares.
GEORGE BICKHAM	One share.
BENJAMIN MASON	One share.
JOHN HOOD	Four shares.
JOHN DONNALDSON, for EDWARD MILNOR	Two shares.
JOHN DONNALDSON, for MARY DONNALDSON	One share.
JOHN and WILLIAM MONTGOMERY	Two shares.
WILLIAM B. HOCKLEY	Two shares.
ISRAEL WHELEN	One share.
EZRA JONES	One share.

Thomas Saltar . .	Four shares.
Leonard Jacoby	One share.
Charles Syng	One share.
John Barclay	One share.
Isaac and Samuel Lewis Wharton .	Six shares.
John Sparhawk .	Four shares.
George Latimer . .	One share.
Pelatiah Webster . . .	Two shares.
Elliston and John Perot	Six shares.
Abram Markoe	Three shares.
Abram Wilt, Jr. . . .	One share.
Henry Hill	Three shares.
Thomas Willing, for the Chevalier De La Luzerne	One share.
Willing, Morris, & Swanwick, for Miss Abby Willing	Three shares.
Jacob L. Swyler, for Jacob Winey .	Five shares.
Thomas Stritch . . .	Two shares.
James B. Nickolls	Two shares.
William Wister	Two shares.
Thomas Willing, for Mrs. Mary Bingham	Three shares.
Andrew Tybout .	One share.
Charles Cooper .	One share.

VI.

SECOND SUBSCRIPTION TO THE NATIONAL BANK CONTINUED AND EXTENDED, 1784.

SECOND subscription to the capital stock of the national bank continued and extended this 1st day of March, 1784, at a general meeting of the stockholders, by whom it was unanimously agreed

That the new subscription shall be extended to the number of four thousand shares, which shall be added to the capital stock of the bank, at four hundred dollars for each share, making in the whole five thousand shares, including both the old and new stock.

That the old, or first stockholders, shall divide the profits of the bank to this day.

That those who have purchased old stock since the last dividend at an advanced price, upon assurance given that the price of the new stock would be held at five hundred dollars, shall have the sum given in advance repaid to them, together with interest at the rate of six per cent. per annum on the whole purchase-money from the day of the transfer, instead of the dividend.

That those who have already subscribed for new stock at five hundred dollars each share shall be repaid an hundred dollars each share, together with interest at the rate of six per cent. per annum on their whole subscription from the time of payment to this day, after which they shall receive dividends in common with all the subscribers, old and new.

THE BANK OF NORTH AMERICA. 141

That all stock subscribed for after this date shall draw a dividend from the day of such subscription respectively.

Wherefore, we, the subscribers, having read the above resolutions, approving, confirming, and hereby agreeing to the same, we sign our names, and opposite thereto affix the number of shares for which we subscribe, having made payment according to the above conditions.

THOMAS WILLING (additional) .	One share.
SAMPSON FLEMING (additional) . .	Thirteen shares.
MORDECAI LEWIS, for LUKE MORRIS	Ten shares.
JOSIAH HEWES	Two shares.
SAMUEL POWEL (additional)	Four shares.
SAMUEL POWEL (additional)	One share.
ANDREW DOZ, for ABRAHAM WAYNE (additional)	One share.
CHARLES WHITE . . .	One share.
JOSIAH COATES	One share.
ROBERT MORRIS (additional)	Two shares.
ROBERT MORRIS, for TENCH TILGHMAN & CO. .	Ten shares.
ELLISTON & JOHN PEROT (additional) .	Two shares.
JOHN SPARHAWK (additional)	One share.
THOMAS WILLING, for ABBY WILLING (additional) .	One share.
THOMAS LOWREY (additional) . .	One share.
MOSES COHEN	Two shares.
JACOB BARGE (additional)	Three shares.
MORDECAI LEWIS & CO. (additional)	One share.
WAGER & HABACHER (additional) .	Two shares.
PHILEMON DICKINSON . .	Twelve shares.
LEVI HOLLINGSWORTH .	Two shares.
W. ALEXANDER & COMP'Y .	Ten shares.
THOMAS SALTAR (additional)	Four shares.
JACOB DOWNING	One share.
SPENCER & MARACHE (additional)	One share.
ISAAC and SAMUEL LEWIS WHARTON (additional) .	Four shares.
CORNELIUS BARNES (additional) . . .	One share.
JOSEPH PENNELL .	Three shares.
WILLIAM CONSTABLE .	Four shares.

18

JOHN JONES .	Twelve shares.
JAMES SLOAN	One share.
CORNELIUS BARNES	One share.
JOHN HOOD (additional)	One share.
PETER LOHRA (additional)	One share.
RICHARD MASON (additional)	One share.
ELEAZER OSWALD .	One share.
THOMAS FRANKLIN	Two shares.
BARBÉ DE MARBOIS	Two shares.
WILLIAM NICHOLS (additional)	One share.
BENJAMIN GIBBS	Two shares.
CASPAR GUYER	One share.
JOSEPH BULLOCK	One share.
JEHU ELDREDGE	One share.
CONRAD WISTER	One share.
BENJAMIN DAVIS, JR.	One share.
BENJAMIN DAVIS, JR.	One share.
BENJAMIN FULLER	Three shares.
JOHN BROWN	Six shares.
THOMAS LEAMING, JR., for THOMAS LEAMING, of Cape May	One share.
JACOB KEEHMLE	One share.
BENJAMIN FULLER .	Seven shares.
MATTHIAS KEELEY	One share.
ROBERT CORREY	One share.
DAVID SELLERS .	One share.
NATHAN SELLERS	One share.
JOHN VAUGHAN (additional), J. DARBY	One share.
BENJAMIN DAVIS, JR., for THOMAS WEST	Two shares.
CASPER SINGER & SON	One share.
WILLIAM B. HOCKLEY, for the six minor children of my deceased sister	One share.
TOWNSEND and JOHN WHITE	One share.
WILLIAM B. HOCKLEY	One share.
FRED'K HEISZ & CO.	Two shares.
LUKE KEATING .	Two shares.
CORNELIUS BARNES	Two shares.
JAMES COX	Two shares.
WILLIAM SYKES	Ten shares.

THE BANK OF NORTH AMERICA. 143

HAYM SALOMON, for JOSHUA MADDOX WALLACE, by order of WILLIAM BRADFORD, ESQ.	Four shares.
JOHN and JAMES OLDDEN	Two shares.
JOSIAH W. and WILLIAM GIBBS, five of these returned cancelled June 4	Five shares.
SAMUEL JACKSON	Two shares.
JACOB DOWNING	One share.
JOHN MING & Co.	One share.
PETER BEDFORD	One share.
WILLIAM and JOHN SITGREAVES	Six shares.
SAMUEL GERRISH, for J. LANGDON, ESQ.	Five shares.
SAMUEL GERRISH, for JOSHUA BRACKET, ESQ.	One share.
JAMES STUART	One share.
ISHMAEL OWENS	One share.
GEORGE LOGAN	Three shares.
PETER KNIGHT	Four shares.
JOHN SWANWICK, on behalf of His Excellency P. J. VAN BERCKEL	Thirteen shares.
JOHN SWANWICK	Eight shares.
SPENCER & MARACHE	Three shares.
JOSEPH SWIFT	Five shares.
WILLIAM and JOHN SPROAT	One share.
PETER THOMSON	One share.
CONRAD GERHARD	Two shares.
PETER W. GALLAUDET	Two shares.
CASPAR W. HAINES	Two shares.
BENJAMIN W. MORRIS, for SARAH WISTAR	Three shares.
EDWARD BURD	Three shares.
COXE & FRAZIER	Two shares.
GEORGE FOX	Fourteen shares.
LEONARD DORSEY	Two shares.
JOHN STEINMETZ	Twenty shares.
SOLOMON LYONS	One share.
REED & FORDE	Three shares.
WILLIAM MCMURTRIE	Twenty shares.
JOSEPH HARRISON, for the Rev. Dr. WHITE	One share.
GEORGE LATIMER, for JAMES BOOTH, ESQ.	One share.
JOHN HOOD	Five shares.
ADAM ZANTZINGER	Five shares.

Robert Bridges	Two shares.
Richard Adams	One share.
Benjamin G. Eyre	One share.
James Craig	Five shares.
John and James Oldden	Two shares.
James C. Fisher	Two shares.
Samuel Howell	Twenty-seven shares.
William Jones	One share.
William Ball	Two shares.
George Fox	One share.
John Steinmetz	Ten shares.
Joseph Cauffman	Two shares.
William Ruibel	Three shares.
William Constable, for William Edgar	Fifty-five shares.
Vardon, Giese & Co.	Five shares.
Jacob Barge, for Elizabeth Gross	One share.
Tench Francis, for Robert Erwin	Two shares.
Henry Voorhees	One share.
John Kidd	One share.
J. Swanwick, on behalf of Tench Tilghman & Co.	Ten shares.
Edward Duffield	One share.
Thomas Fitzsimons, for Anna Maria Clifton	One share.
Nathaniel Falconer, for General Mifflin	Eleven shares.
Nathaniel Falconer, for Rebecca Morris	One share.
Pragers, Liebaert & Co.	Ten shares.
Thomas Penrose, for Thomas Penrose, Jr.	One share.
Archibald Gamble, for Jane Cannon	One share.
Henry Hill, for James Jacks, Esq., of Lancaster	One share.
Benjamin Fuller	Five shares.
Donnaldson & Coxe	Twenty shares.
Ann Powell, by John Wilson	One share.
Tench Francis, for the Honorable Arthur Lee	Fourteen shares.
John Jones, for Thomas Jones	Seven shares.
Nathaniel Falconer, for Mary Bickley	Three shares.
Collins & Truxtun	Two shares.
Abram Markoe	Four shares.
Israel Morris, Jr., for Luke Morris	Four shares.
John Angus	Four shares.
Benjamin Fuller	Four shares.

THE BANK OF NORTH AMERICA. 145

JAMES HUNTER.	One share.
DAVID KENNEDY.	One share.
JOHN F. MIFFLIN	One share.
JOHN NIXON,) Executors to estate of M. ROGERS, J. M. NESBITT,) late of this city, deceased	Three shares.
MAGNUS MILLER	Three shares.
FREDERICK GREINER	One share.
TENCH FRANCIS, for Honorable ARTHUR LEE	One share.
MICHAEL HILLEGAS, for Captain EDWARD NORTH	Two shares.
JACOB LAVERSWYLER, for CATHARINE LAVERSWYLER	One share.
THOMAS PARKE, for HANNAH LLOYD	Two shares.
TENCH FRANCIS, for the Honorable ARTHUR LEE	Two shares.
PETER WHITESIDE, for WALLACE, JOHNSON & MUIR.	Two shares.
WILLIAM BELL	Fifteen shares.
JOHN BROWN & SONS, for ALEXANDER PORTER	Twelve shares.
JOHN BROWN & SONS, for ALEXANDER PORTER	One share.
JOHN WHARTON, as one of the executors of the Honorable THOMAS WHARTON, ESQ., deceased, on behalf of the four minor children of his deceased brother by his first wife, SUSANNAH, viz.: LLOYD, KEARNEY, MOORE, and SARAH WHARTON	Five shares.
GEORGE SCHAFFNER	Five shares.
NATHANIEL FALCONER, for General THOMAS MIFFLIN	Two shares.
EDWARD BURD	Two shares.
TENCH FRANCIS, for the Honorable ARTHUR LEE	One share.
BENJAMIN CHEW	Three shares.
MICHAEL SHUBART, for the GERMAN SOCIETY	Three shares.
JACOB LAVERWSYLER, for JACOB WINEY	Four shares.
BENJAMIN FULLER, as one of the executors of WILLIAM WEST, deceased, on behalf of the five minor children of said WILLIAM WEST, viz.: WILLIAM HODGE, JAMES, BENJAMIN FULLER, ANNIE, and HELEN WEST, three shares each, making	Fifteen shares.
RICHARD FOOTMAN, for the estate of PETER CARMICK, deceased	One share.
BENJAMIN FULLER, for DAVID HAYFIELD CONYNGHAM	One share.
CATHARINE LARDNER, by WILLIAM LARDNER	One share.

JOHN OLDDEN, for SAMUEL OLDDEN	One share.
T. F., for SAMSON FLEMING, by order of THOMAS FITZSIMONS	Two shares.
ARTHUR LEE	One share.
MATTHIAS HARRISON, for THOMAS MIFFLIN, ESQ.	One share.
ISAAC WARNER	Six shares.
THOMAS HARRISON	Two shares.
THOMAS HARRISON	One share.
CONSTABLE, RUCKER & CO., by GARRETT COTTRINGER	Twenty shares.
G. FOWLER	Five shares.
CASPAR GUYER	Two shares.
MARY TUCKER, by WILLIAM SMITH	Four shares.
WILLIAM FOOT, by WILLIAM SMITH, for the use of two minor daughters of the deceased Mr. THOMAS A. BURCH	Four shares.
THOMAS, SAMUEL, and MIERS FISHER	Ten shares.
THOMAS HARRISON	One share.
ALEXANDER STUART	Eight shares.
WILLIAM B. HOCKLEY	Two shares.
WILLIAM RUIBEL	One share.
JOHN KIDD	Two shares.
BENJAMIN FULLER, for MARGARET STOCKER	Eight shares.
BENJAMIN FULLER, for MARGARET STOCKER, JR.	Eight shares.
WILLIAM B. HOCKLEY	One share.
NATHAN SELLERS	One share.
DAVID SELLERS	One share.
RICHARD BACHE, for WILLIAM TEMPLE FRANKLIN, ESQ.	Eleven shares.
J. SWANWICK, on behalf of Mr. ARNOUD DAVID VAN LENNEP	Ten shares.
SAMUEL SMITH	Twelve shares.
JOHN GRAY, for SARAH FITZSIMONS (widow)	One share.
JOHN KIDD, for MARY FOULKE	Two shares.
JOHN LUKENS	Four shares.
JOHN JAY	One share.
OUSRAY PAINNIERE	Two shares.
JEREMIAH WARDER, PARKER & CO.	Four shares.
GARRETT COTTRINGER, on behalf of GEORGE C. ANTHON	Six shares.

JOHN ROSS, for Mrs. DORCAS MONTGOMERY	One share.
JAMES READ, for GEORGE READ	Two shares.
THOMAS FITZSIMONS, for MATTHIAS OOSTER .	Twenty-five shares.
THOMAS FITZSIMONS, for HENDRICK HOVY	Twenty shares.
CURTIS CLAY, for Mrs. ANN CLAY . . .	One share.
J. SWANWICK, for G. K. VAN HOODENDERP .	Ten shares.
MORDECAI LEWIS, for JAN DEKNATEL . .	Three shares.
MORDECAI LEWIS, for HERMAN ANGELKOT	Two shares.

VII.

CORRESPONDENCE WITH THE COMPTROLLER OF THE CURRENCY AS TO THE RETENTION BY THE BANK OF THE NAME OF THE "BANK OF NORTH AMERICA" ON BECOMING A NATIONAL BANK.

Thomas Smith, Esq., President, to Hon. Hugh McCulloch, Comptroller:

PHILADELPHIA, October 28, 1864.

Proposing that the Bank of North America should become a national bank, and suggesting that it should retain the title of the "Bank of North America," without the usual prefix of "National."

Hon. Hugh McCulloch, Comptroller, to Thomas Smith, Esq., President:

WASHINGTON, October 29, 1864.

DEAR SIR,—Your favor of the 28th inst. is received. Such has been the history and such the relations of the Bank of North America to the General Government, that it seems to be eminently proper that in its reorganization and rejuvenation under the National Currency Act, it should assume as its title "The National Bank of North America." Every State bank hitherto changed into a national association has taken, in connection with its former name, the word "National," and I should regret it if the oldest and most loyal of all of them should be unwilling to indicate *by its title* its relations to the national banking system of the National Government.

In order to make the change, you must obtain the consent of the owners of two-thirds of the capital stock of your bank, and, if you advise it, I do not believe that a single one of them will hesitate to assent to the introduction of the word "National" into the title. Please let me hear from you on this point.

I do not now say that I shall decline sanctioning the reorganization of your bank under its present title alone. If I do it, it will be against my own judgment and with extreme reluctance.

There was, I think, well-founded objection to the "numeral system" of Mr. Chase, but of the 561 banks organized under the national system not one has objected to the word "National" as a part of its title, and I do not believe that, upon reflection, you will.

Some parts of your letter please me so much that I would publish them if I felt at liberty to do so.

I forward you a half dozen sets of Forms, etc.

                Very truly yours,

                      H. McCulloch, Comptroller.

Thomas Smith, Esq., President Bank of North America, Philadelphia.

Thomas Smith, Esq., President, to Hugh McCulloch, Esq., Comptroller:

                              Philadelphia, November 1, 1864.

Hon. Hugh McCulloch, Comptroller of the Currency.

Dear Sir,—Your valued favor of the 29th is at hand. Wishing to avoid the use of your valuable time in a matter of so little moment as the addition of the word "National" in the name of this bank, I am compelled to do so because there is so much feeling about *any* change of name with the stockholders and directors, arising principally from the fact that its present is its old *national* name given to it by Congress in 1781, retained by it, after *much violent* opposition, in confirmatory charters had from Delaware, Massachusetts, and Pennsylvania, the same political heresy of State rights being then, as now, rampant.

There is no similarity between this and any other bank, either State or National.

First. We hold the national charter, December 31, 1781, which has never been abandoned or relinquished, but, in consequence of the partisan opposition to the bank, this charter was confirmed by the three States in which its business was chiefly done. No new charter was given or made. It was simply confirmatory of the charter made by the United States, which confirmatory charters by this State have been renewed (being limited in duration) as they expired. The original charter is perpetual.

The great merit of the corporation and pride has always been its national character. We have it in brass in the building and printed on the notes. In July, 1862, we passed, and published in the papers, a resolution, a copy of which I inclose. We loaned all we had to the Government when they wanted it, and the timid said it was imprudent to do so, and we have and hold two and a half times the amount of the capital in United States securities now, and intend to do so. The national banks are generally organized to benefit the stockholders, and for that purpose only. This bank was created avowedly to aid the United States. It fulfilled its mission, and then went on prosperously, filled with the pride of that mission.

These are some of the reasons for asking permission to retain our national name of "The Bank of North America." The matter has been thoroughly canvassed by the directors, and I will frankly state that I heartily agree with them in pressing the request. With a personal interview, and the documents in our possession, I feel you would say we were right. At the same time we shall do nothing, however small, to detract from the strength of the nation in this her struggle for existence. And we believe the national bank system to be one very great element of success and strength. Should you determine that we cannot change without an alteration of name, please inform me in relation to it, our arrangements all being made for the old name. In the mean time, I inclose you specimens of the issue of the notes of the bank, if you are at all curious in such matters, the issues of the Revolution, the war with Great Britain, and the Rebellion. They are genuine, and good for redemption at any time.

Awaiting your leisure to hear from you, I am,

Respectfully, your obedient servant,

THOMAS SMITH, President.

The same to the same:

PHILADELPHIA, November 11, 1864.

H. MCCULLOCH, ESQ., Comptroller of the Currency.

DEAR SIR,—Your favor of the 4th was duly received. I should have felt much relieved by something to warrant the belief that you would sanction the old name. The meeting of stockholders is on Monday next, and it is by no means certain that the requisite number of two-thirds can be obtained at all. The election has demonstrated that Uncle Sam can take care of himself now, and there is, therefore, no necessity for any little moral support, besides there are several Banks of North America, and after a time there may be the same number of *National* Banks of North America.

I can, if you desire, send you a commendation from the other banks for our old name. The notes I sent you are to be retained; we have other specimens of the same kind.

Respectfully, your obedient servant,

THOMAS SMITH, President.

The same to the same:

PHILADELPHIA, November 15, 1864.

HON. H. McCULLOCH, Comptroller, etc.

DEAR SIR,—The stockholders of this bank have voted authority to its directors to change from State to National. Our desire is to retain its present name in the organization certificate,—

"The Bank of North America."

Will you be pleased to inform me if this will meet your approval in order to avoid the trouble and vexation attending a failure? Referring to my previous letters on this matter, and awaiting your reply,

I am your obedient servant,

THOMAS SMITH, President.

We are progressing slowly with obtaining the consent of two-thirds of the stockholders.

In consequence of the foregoing correspondence, and at the request of the presidents of most of the Philadelphia banks, the Comptroller of the Currency at length consented to allow "The Bank of North America" to retain its original title, without the prefix "National," on becoming a national bank.—See *ante*, page 118.

VIII.

DIVIDENDS PAID BY THE BANK OF NORTH AMERICA FROM 1782 TO THE PRESENT TIME.

Year	Dividend		Year	Dividend		Year	Dividend	
1782	8¾	per cent.	1809	9	per cent.			
1783	14½	"	1810	9½	"			
1784	13½	"	1811	9	"			
1785	6	"	1812	9	"			
1786	6	"	1813	10	"			
1787	6	"	1814	10	"			
1788	6½	"	1815	10	"			
1789	7	"	1816	10	"			
1790	7	"	1817	10	"			
1791	13½	"	1818	10	"			
1792	12½	"	1819	9	"			
1793	12	"	1820	6½	"			
1794	12	"	1821	6	"			
1795	12	"	1822	6	"			
1796	12	"	1823	6	"			
1797	12	"	1824	6	"			
1798	12	"	1825	6	"			
1799	11	"	1826	6	"			
1800	10	"	1827	4	"			
1801	10	"	1828	5	"			
1802	10	"	1829	5	"			
1803	9	"	1830	5	"			
1804	9	"	1831	5	"			
1805	9	"	1832	5	"			
1806	9	"	1833	6	"			
1807	9	"	1834	6	"			
1808	9	"	1835	7	"			

1836 .	7	per cent.	1859 .	12	per cent.
1837 .	6	"	1860 .	9	"
1838 .	6	"	1861 .	6	"
1839 .	3	"	1862 .	10	"
1840 .	9	"	1863 .	12	"
1841 .	2½	"	1864 .	12	"
1842 .	One cent.		1865 .	31	"
1843 .	6	per cent.	1866 .	22½	"
1844 .	8	"	1867 .	30	"
1845 .	8	"	1868 .	22½	"
1846 .	8	"	1869 .	20	"
1847 .	10	"	1870 .	20	"
1848 .	15	"	1871 .	20	"
1849 .	12	"	1872 .	20	"
1850 .	15	"	1873 .	20	"
1851 .	15	"	1874 .	20	"
1852 .	15	"	1875 .	20	"
1853 .	15	"	1876 .	20	"
1854 .	15	"	1877 .	16	"
1855 .	15	"	1878 .	16	"
1856 .	15	"	1879 .	16	"
1857 .	11	"	1880 .	16	"
1858 .	10	"			

The amount to credit of surplus and profit and loss, January 1, 1860, was $288,361.81

There was to credit of the same accounts on January 1, 1881 1,100,000.00

Showing a gain of $811,638.19

During the same period there have been paid to the stockholders dividends amounting to . . 3,700,000.00

Showing total profits, being over 451 per cent. $4,511,638.19

www.ingramcontent.com/pod-product-compliance
Lightning Source LLC
Chambersburg PA
CBHW020843160426
43192CB00007B/761